Dreams, Screams, and Jellybeans!

Poems for All Ages

Poems by Kevin J. Brougher
Drawings by Shannon Grogan-Brochu

Missing Piece Press, LLC
TUCSON - ARIZONA

Dreams, Screams, and JellyBeans!
Poems for All Ages

Text Copyright © 2003, 2018 by Kevin J. Brougher
Illustrations copyright © 2003 Shannon Grogan-Brochu

All rights reserved.
No part of this book may be reproduced by any means
without the written permission of the publisher.

Printed in the United States of America

ISBN 0-9703729-2-2

Missing Piece Press is publisher of books and games.
Other publications:

Thinking Books
Thinklers! 1
Thinklers! 2
Thinklers! 3
Science Stumpers
Algebra Summary Sheets
Number Wonders
History Mysteries
Children's Books
Reindolphins
Board Games
WHEW!
ShanJari
Card Games
TooT!
Blam!
Word Nerd
State Debate
Dice Games
DICE Blam!

Missing Piece Press, LLC
TUCSON - ARIZONA
MissingPiecePress.com

Table of Contents

Dedication	6
Dreams, Screams, and Jelly Beans	7
Plan	8
Paste Tense	9
Baseball Bumble	10
Thief	11
The Ump	11
Ever?	12
Okay	13
Roof Top	14
I Scream	15
Hello, My Friend	16
Lion	17
Boo	18
Smart Kid	19
Brother	20
Advice	21
High Dive Dilemma	22
Jimmy Zat	23
Wishing	23
Salsa	24
Gummy Grin	24
Contest	25
Friends	26
Life's Too Short	27
Bye	28
Life's an Adventure	28
Dinner	29
Don't Lose It	30
Two-Headed Dog	31
Epitaph	32
Blue Lagoon	32
Johnny Joe	33
Rip City	34
Sandwich Club	35
How Would You React?	36
Joy	37
Under Talk	37
On Aging	38
Room Cleaning	39
No Luck	40
Ketchup	41
Too Sick	41
Humpty	42
Humpty 2	42
Wise Teacher	43
Good / Bad	44
Baby Sit	45
Believe	46
Doughnuts	47
Would You Rather	47
Polite	48
Talk	49
Rain	50
Question	50
Jack and Jill	51
?????	51
Tarantula	52
Grandma's Gone	53
Brand New Marker	54
$$$$$	55
Python	55
Careful	56
Show Me	57
Things	58
To the Teacher	58
Plans	59
Be Nice	59
The Scare	60
I Can?	61
I Feel Like Playing in Mud	62
My Pet Hen	63
Happy Hydrant	63
Get Down	64
Porcupine	64
Rude	65
Cannot Sleep	66
Laugh	66
Dogs	67
Doggone	67
Dog Decisions	68
Cats	69
Smart Dog	70
Snake	70
Horses	71
Walrus	71
Parakeet	72

Pet Problems	72	Homonym Scholar	110
New Kitten	73	Sword Swallower	111
A Gaggle of Geese	74	Dare Devil	112
Horse	75	Room Gloom	112
Spider	76	Magic Bro	113
The Chicken and the Human	77	Not-So-Funny Bone	114
Better Pets	78	Secret	115
My Way	79	Dinner Joke	115
Too Much	79	Mealtime	116
Don't Be Afraid	80	Dad's Beard	117
Good Learners	81	Mom's Working	118
No Artist	81	Lollipop	118
Hair	83	Allowance	119
Golf	83	Still Me?	120
Wish	84	Try	121
Wedgy	85	Listen	122
Bath	86	Step on Crack	123
Sweet Lesson	87	Morning Chore	124
Move It	87	Telephone Moan	124
Back to Bed	88	Stone Soup	125
Hugs	89	No Twin	125
Pumpkin Time	90	Diner Dilemma	126
Christmas Wish	91	Broccoli	126
The Season	91	Green Bananas	127
Advice for Santa	92	Sneezy	128
Holiday News	92	Sick	128
Tis the Season	93	Hungry	129
The Christmas Tree	94	Room Clean	130
Decorating	95	The Chase	131
Early Gift	96	Curious	132
Slow Going	97	Gone	132
Vomit	98	Glue	133
Rules	99	Beans	134
Plan to Plan	99	The Shot	135
Cloud 9	100	Fried	135
Donny's Desk	101	Don't	136
Teacher's Last Lecture	101	What We Like…	137
Crisis in Class	102	The Best Cake	138
Love & Lies	103	Backward Billy	139
Help?	104	Idol	140
Homework	104	Shaved	140
The Greatest Fault	105	Fishing Trip	141
No Hair	106	Garbage	141
Germs	106	What a Kid	142
Success	107	But Dad	143
Diet	108	Jelly Fish	144
Listen	108	Rest	144
Zukes	109	Too Neat	145

Big Belly Bob…	146
Oh, Mary	147
Mother's Plea	147
What the Boss Says	148
Pie Spy	148
Thumb	149
Engineer	150
Crayons	151
Plot of Land	152
Dino	152
Picture Perfect Patty	153
Nella	154
Little Brother	155
The Comma	155
Shopping Stress	156
Revenge	157
Get Up!	158
Why I Like You	159
Friends	159
The Face	160
Rich	160
Are We There Yet?	161
Parade	162
Gifts	162
Crybaby	163
Time for Me	164
Early Bird	164
Mary's Pets	165
Darla	166
Inch by Inch	167
Seattle Dreams	167
Choices	168
What I've Got	169
Minds	169
Shorties	170
Backward Poet	171
Good News	171
Forever	171
Diet	171
No Sunshine	172
Puzzle	172
Farmer	172
Word to the Wise	173
Meal Time	173
Sleep	173
Weatherman	174
Huh?	174
Fool	175
Brother	175
Uncle William	175
Night Out	176
Pony	176
Dead Sea	176
Not Feeling Well	177
Stay Home Dad	177
Left Gone	177
The END	178
INDEX	179
Other Publications	183

Dreams, Screams, and Jellybeans!

Poems for All Ages

Poems by Kevin J. Brougher
Drawings by Shannon Grogan-Brochu

Dedication

For those of you who listened,
For those of you who cared,
For those of you who took the time,
To let me think and share,
For those of you who work with kids,
And, share my point of view,
For those who do believe in me,
This book....it is for you!

Dreams, Screams, and Jellybeans

*Some poems that you'll read in here
I hope will make you dream.
I'm pretty sure that others
are bound to make you scream.
I wrote them both for young and old
and, even in-betweens.
So, read them with some popcorn
or, a bowl of jellybeans!
But, because I took the time
to think them up and type 'em
I hope you read them all,
And ......really, really like 'em!*

PLAN

I have a plan for you, I do.
I'll share it with you now.
Please follow these directions.
Here's what to do and how.
Start to read this book and when...
the pages finally end...
BURN this book, then, find a store,
and buy the book... AGAIN! ☺

Past Tense!

Past tense they say, is the proper way,
   to show that something's been done.
So, after you say it, then you have said it.
   See, it truly is fun!
For after you've run, you've ran,
   after you've spit, you've spat.
This amazing procedure,
  that's taught by a teacher,
   can even change this to that!
Yes, after you fly, you have flown.
    After you sew, you have sewn.
And, after you throw, a ball to and fro,
   then you can say you have thrown.
Now, after you tell,
     you've told,
after you sell,
     you've sold.
You can do this all day,
but, in warning I'll say,
  if you do it too much it gets old.
But, if you fail a test, you flunk it.
   If you sink a ship, you've sunk it.
And, if sitting at home thinking,
   who could think of this poem,
     I'm proud to say, **I THUNK IT!**

BASEBALL BUMBLE

Crack, goes the bat, and my legs begin to shake.
Then I hear the crowd yell.......
"RUN, FOR HEAVEN'S SAKE!"
So, I'm heading off to 1st, when I hear a little POP.
It's the button on my pants but, I'm not about to stop!
Then on my way to 2nd, I feel a little breeze.
I take a glance down, and my pants are at my knees!
Now, on my way to 3rd, I start to feel the heat,
'cause, now my pants are hanging....down upon my feet!
I made it safe to home but, the sight was rather rare,
'Cause on that summer day........
...I forgot my underwear!

Thief

My mommy says, "Don't be a thief,
'cause stealing things is wrong!"
She needn't fret, I promised her,
"I've known that all along."
But, still the look of stress and grief,
was painted on her face.
Just because I shared with her,
that I had stole third base.

The Ump

Baseball is my favorite sport.
I've been to many games.
<u>ONE</u> thing, that I' ve learned quite well...
...the UMP has lots of names!

Ever?

Have you ever seen a seahorse,
who didn't like to swim?
Or, an African hyena,
who didn't like to grin?
Have you ever seen a baby,
who didn't ever cry?
I'll tell you once,
I'll tell you twice....NOT I!

OKAY

While running on the playground
I fell and scraped my knee.
While eating lunch, I spilt my milk...
for everyone to see.
While playing on the monkey bars
I popped my biggest blister.
My best friend hugged my girlfriend and then....
and THEN, he kissed her!
I flunked my test in history class.
My pen ran out of ink.
I left my shoes out in the rain
and, now they sure do stink.
A baseball slipped right through my glove
and hit me in the nose.
I ran from third and slid to home
and jammed most all my toes.
My mother asked, "How are you, Son?
How was you day today?"
I thought about it hard and long
and then I said,
.....''O-K.''

ROOF TOP

I'm going to bed on the roof tonight.
    I'm going to wish on the stars.
I'll look out over the city.
    I'll look at the planes and the cars.
I'm going to bed on the roof tonight.
    I might find it too hard to sleep,
'cause this roof is a little bit creaky,
    and more than a little too...S
                                  T
                              E
                                  E
                                      P!

I Scream!

My ice cream's on the sidewalk.
The cone is down there too.
There's nothing like an accident
To make me feel so blue!
The sidewalk is quite hot today.
I'd better do this quick.
And, get down on that sidewalk
and lick, lick, lick, lick lick!

Hello, My Friend.

Hello, my friend! How are you?
    That's all I asked that day.
I never thought my friend,
    would have so much to say.
She shared with me her problems,
    her sorrows and her woes.
She talked about her aching back
    and fungus in her toes.
She discussed the rainy weather.   She debated politics.
    She divulged the plot and story, of Hollywood's new flicks.
She revealed family secrets.   She gave investment tips.
    She lectured for an hour, on TV censorship.
Then, as my friend was leaving, she said, "Let's keep in touch!"
    I'll have to think about it, 'cause my friend...She talks too much!

Lion

I slipped into the lion cage
to get a closer look.
At first I didn't have a fear,
but, then my body shook.
The lion looked and smiled at me.
I figured.... he's a grinner!
Either that, or could it be,
he thinks.........that I'm his dinner!

BOO

On Halloween, I met a ghost.
      We sat and talked awhile.
He said that scaring little kids
      was really not his style.
He said he really didn't like
      this thing called trick-or-treating.
How could parents, let their kids
      do all that candy eating?
Then, he looked at me and smiled,
      and said, "Well, how 'bout you?"
I slowly turned and scrunched my face
      and then I shouted, "BOOO!"
He yelled and screamed and flew away.
      I think I now can boast,
that I'm the only one I know...
      who's ever scared a ghost!

Smart Kid

I found a set of Christmas lights.
I taped them to my clothes.
I put one in each ear and then...
I glued one to my nose.
I got a long extension cord,
Plugged it in and walked around.
I got a lot of funny looks,
But, didn't see one frown.
I did this for one reason, friends,
and to my heart's delight,
I finally heard some people say...
"Boy, that kid is bright!"

BROTHER

*My brother never showers.
He never combs his hair.
He never takes a bath.
He doesn't seem to care.
My brother really stinks.
That's why I've always known,
that when he stands in line –
he'll always stand alone!*

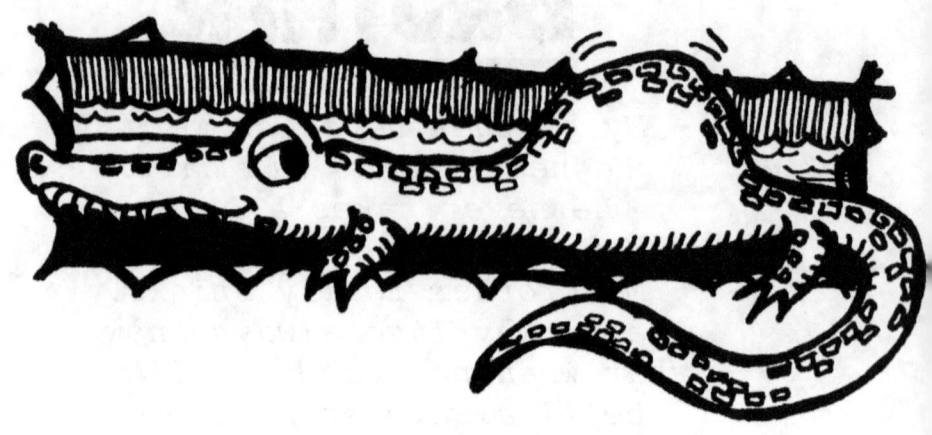

Advice

I wouldn't tell an alligator,
"No, I'd rather not."
And, I wouldn't sneeze upon him,
and shower him with snot.
I wouldn't pull his tail,
I wouldn't call him names.
I wouldn't say, he couldn't play,
or beat him at a game.
This...is my advice.
But, you'll have to thank me later,
When I find a safe way out…
from the inside of this gator!

High Dive Dilemma

I stood out on the high dive board
    and looked down at the pool.
With shaking legs and sweating brow,
    I felt like such a fool.
But, I found a burst of bravery
    and made the grandest dive.
It wasn't quite a perfect ten,
    but, still...I was alive!
And, though my goal was finally met,
    I now felt destitute.
For in that dive, I hate to say...
    I lost my swimming suit!

JIMMY ZAT

Jimmy Zat, the pack rat,
   saved most everything.
He'd save a rock. He'd save a clock.
   He'd save a 10 cent ring.
He'd save a game. He'd save a book.
   He'd save a pawn. He'd save a rook.
He'd save a bottle. He'd save a can.
   He'd save a pot. He'd save a pan.
He'd save it all, but all too soon,
   Jimmy Zat...ran out of ROOM!

Wishing

I wish I had a wish to wish.
   I wish I had a dream.
I wish I had a sister,
   who didn't like to scream!
I wish I had a smaller nose,
   that sits upon my face.
I wish I was an astronaut,
   flying into space.
I wish I'd win the lottery,
   or, had the Midas touch.
I'll tell you what my parents think,
   They think I wish too much!

SALSA
My eyes are red.
I'm sweating, too.
My throat must be on fire!
You said the salsa
wasn't hot.
I'd say that you're a liar!

Gummy Grin

I lost a tooth
    the other day.
I woke up with a dollar!
That made me smile.
    That made me jump.
That made me hoot and holler!
I had a plan –
    it seemed quite good.
        But, mother took a fall.
When she saw my toothless mouth today,
    ...for I had pulled them all!

CONTEST

Today we had a contest.
The <u>oldest</u> one would win.
I thought I just might win this year!
I tried to hide the grin.
But, when the final name was called,
Or, so it would appear,
BILLY won the contest.
He beats me every year!

FRIEND

No one seems to play with me
    (It's true I sometimes cheat.)
No one seems to say to me,
    "Hey, you're really neat!"
I think because I'm kind of mean
    No one says I'm fun.
I guess it's true, to have a friend
    You have to learn to be one!

LIFE'S TOO SHORT

Life's too short, to always complain
at the slightest problem, or the smallest pain.
Life's too short, to fight with a friend;
as soon as it starts, I think it should end.
Life's too short, to spend your time poutin',
so take a deep breath, and climb up a mountain.
Life is too short, to be serious all day.
It's important to rest - it's important to play.
Life is too short, to be sad or be mad.
So, wake up today, and decide to be glad.
Yes, life goes by quickly, it ends much too soon.
So, set your goals now, and shoot for the moon!

Bye

I think I want, upon my grave,
when I do finally die,
Some simple words, like
"rest in peace."
Or, maybe just – "Good-bye!"

LIFE'S AN ADVENTURE

Try a new flavor, a new drink, a new dish.
Try a new spice, if that's what you wish.
Try a new sport. Try a new game.
Try it for fun, not fortune or fame.
Learn a new language. Learn a new song.
Learn to stay fit. Learn to be strong.
Change how you look. Change your career.
The worst thing you face,
can't hurt you; it's fear.
Experience the thrill of taking a hike,
    to the top of a mountain,
        it's a beautiful sight.
Do what you dream.
    Give it your best.
Give it your all.
Accept nothing less.
Yes, challenge yourself,
    start now, don't stall.
For, life is an adventure........
    or nothing at all!

DINNER

I sat down for spaghetti,
    took a noodle - slurped it in.
I looked around the table,
    but, I didn't see ONE grin.
"What's wrong?", I asked politely.
    "What's wrong for heaven's sake?"
One shy guy, his reply,
    "I think you ate a snake!"
My eyes got wide. I held my side.
    I couldn't help but squirm.
But, then he said, "Don't worry, Fred.
    I'm wrong ...
        ...it was a worm!"

Don't Lose It

If you take the fuse out
of a bomb,
the bomb would be DE-fused.
DEforestation happens,
when our forests
we do lose.
Take away the frost,
you DEfrost.
That's kind of neat.
But, if you are DEfeated,
What happens to your feet?!

Two-Headed Dog

A 2-headed dog.... is what I have,
I know that you might not believe me.
But, have him I do, and he has me too,
and I know that he never will leave me.
The heads are quite normal - nothing unique.
One, on each end of his body.
He knows where he's going.
He knows where he's been.
It's hard for my dog to be naughty.
But, what is unique,
when the heads turn around,
they look at themselves face to face.
With the look in their eyes,
they say with a sigh,
"I'm sorry... there's NO tail to chase."

Epitaph

When almost dead,
my epitaph
will be my last endeavor.
When it's read,
I hope they laugh,
and say,
"He *SURE* was clever!"

BLUE LAGOON

While fishing in the Blue Lagoon
 I caught a scary creature.
With warts and horns and slimy skin,
 and eyes just like a teacher!
It must have weighed five thousand pounds.
 Its lips began to smack.
He looked at me. I looked at him.
 ....I think I'll throw him back!

Johhny Joe

I'm Johhny Joe the jogger.
    I've jogged for three years straight!
I use to weigh 500 pounds.
    (I'd say that's overweight!)
But, now I weigh just 50 pounds.
    (That's when I'm fully dressed!)
I stand just barely 4 feet tall.
    (My backbone has compressed!)
My teeth are green. My body's sore,
    My hair looks like a mop.
I'm Johhny Joe the jogger, and
    I think it's time to stop!

Rip City

Someone ripped their pants!
Everyone could tell.
The sound, you couldn't miss it.
We thought that this was swell!
We giggled and we laughed.
But, my smile did decline.
When it came to my attention,
that the pants that ripped...
..were mine!

SANDWICH CLUB

There was a man, all dressed in cheese -
    another dressed in bread.
A lady had some lettuce on -
    she wore it on her head.
A couple kids wore ketchup.
    One had mustard pants.
One man had a plan to do...
    a sliced bologna dance.
They called themselves the sandwich club,
    A funny kind of group.
They asked if I could stay awhile,
    for I was dressed ... as SOUP!

How Would You React?

If we took away an elephants, thick and wrinkled skin
    and took away his trunk, and his silly grin,
would he still be an elephant? Should we change his name?
    Could we call an elephant, an elephant, if he didn't look the same?
And, what about the skunk? If we took away his stink
    then, covered up his stripe...do you know what I think?
I think we wouldn't recognize, this animal so well known.
    But, at least when we did smell him, we wouldn't moan and groan!
And, imagine if you will, a solid color zebra.
    Or, a pink and purple penguin, or a 5 foot long amoebae.
Or, what about a hippo, that's as skinny as a deer?
    Or, a Caribbean turtle, with a shell that's crystal clear?
Would a snake be a snake, if covered with dark hair?
    If a bear had scaly skin, I bet you'd surely stare.
And, you'd stare at a whale, that walked upon the land
    and said "How do you do?" and kindly shook your hand!
And, if ducks were rainbow colored, it would be a pretty sight...
    but, you just might mistake them, for a high flying kite.
And, if rabbits were not furry, and didn't hop at all,
    or giraffes had webbed feet, and were only four feet tall.
Or, what if monkeys "oinked" and pigs swung in trees,
    and DOGS had the stingers...instead of bumblebees?
What would we do, what would we say? How would we all react?
    Well, at least I got you thinking. I'm sure... that is a fact!

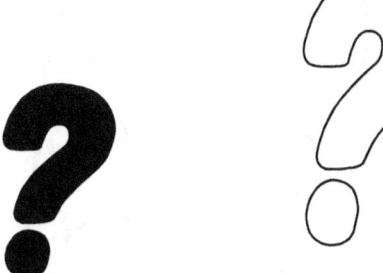

Joy

Kids can fill your life with joy -
   and yet I must confess,
  I look around my house each day,
   they sure can make a mess!

Under Talk

If underpants could talk, I'd bet,
   they'd say they LIKE not being wet.
They'd say, "Don't eat those beans and such!
   And please don't, please don't scratch so much!"
And, if they ever sang a song,
   they'd sing, "You've worn me much too long!
Change me! Change me! Change me, DO!
   It's TOUGH, being underpants for you!"

ON AGING

You know you are old, when there's hair in your ears.
    You know you are old, when it's harder to hear.
You know you are old, when your knees start to wobble,
    after playing a game, you practically hobble.
There's spots on your skin, and lines on your face.
    Your hair starts to gray, it's such a disgrace.
Your muscles get flabby, they're not as strong as before,
    And, when sitting in church, it's not long till you snore.
There's one last thing, I'll say in this talk,
    I think that...
        What was that...
            Good golly...
                I FORGOT!

Room Cleaning

I wish my room would clean itself.
    That's what I wish each day.
I wish my room would clean itself,
    so I could go and play.
It's always such a messy room.
    The floor is hard to see.
If you were here to see the room,
    I'm sure you would agree.
I wish my room would clean itself.
    But, maybe I could find...
A friend to clean my room for me.
    ....Do you mind?

N♥ LU♥CK

I put a sign, upon my back.
It advertised free kisses.
If ever there was a brilliant plan,
I'd have to say that this is!
I hiked around the city streets.
I covered many acres.
But, this plan I had, it made me mad.
There just weren't any takers.

Ketchup

I need a little Ketchup.
So in my hand I clutch,
The bottle and I shake it.
Oops!........too much!

Too Sick

I'm much too sick to clean my room.
    I'm much too sick to sweep.
I'll have to watch cartoons all day.
    Or, maybe I'll just sleep.
I cannot feed the dog or cat.
    But, huh? What's that you say?
My friends are at the front door - now?
    Oh, Mom! Can I go play?

HUMPTY

Humpty Dumpty sat on a wall.
Humpty Dumpty had a great fall.
All the king's horses
and all the king's men,
couldn't put Humpty together again.
But, whoever heard, of an egg as a king?
Though, the subjects were surely grief stricken.
If he didn't fall off, the subjects would scoff,
if that king had changed to a chicken!

HUMPTY 2

Humpty Dumpty sat on a wall.
Humpty Dumpty had a great fall.
All the king's horses and all the king's men,
couldn't put Humpty together again.
But, that's OK, 'cause that old King
he talked so much - he rambled!
Now, he'll never talk again
'cause Humpty, well....
he's scrambled!

Wise Teacher

Good morning, boys & girls.
(Sit down - shut up - be good!)
Please, take out your math books.
(Do it quick! Just like you should!)
Billy, please stop talking.
(What are you? Deaf and Dumb?)
Can you answer the first problem?
(Let me guess, your brain is numb!)
Susie, try to focus.
(What a sleepy head!)
Yes...A wise and caring teacher,
   leaves many thoughts unsaid.

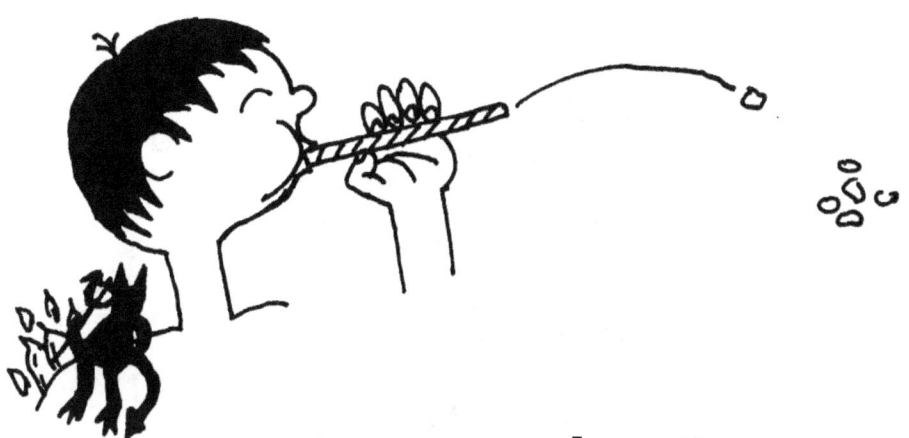

Good / Bad

I can't quite seem to spell those words.
I can't quite seem to think.
At math I struggle everyday.
At history, I stink.
But, my spit wads are the very best.
They're stickier than most.
I can hit a dime, ten feet away.
Well, that is what I boast.
I'm talented at making sounds
That make my friends all giggle.
When there's work to do, I know it's true,
I always seem to wiggle.
This all is quite confusing
And, I've never understood,
Why I'm <u>good</u> at doing <u>bad</u> things,
And, <u>bad</u> at being <u>good</u>!

Baby Sit

My baby-sitter sat on me.
    I couldn't move a bit.
All she did, that whole night long,
    was sit, sit, sit, sit, sit!
My mommy didn't understand,
    I'll have to reprimand her.
A baby-sitter's not for me!
    I want a *baby-stander!*

Believe

*To be someone special,
believe that you are.
THAT'S, the first step you must take.
It's been proven my friends,
if you believe in yourself,
the results can really be great.
So, set your goals high.
Work hard and you'll find,
your dreams will one day come true.
And, I'd love to take credit,
for all of your work
but, success is dependent ...on you!*

DOUGHNUTS

   I ate a bunch of doughnuts
     that were sitting in some bowls.
Now, I'm feeling empty
  'Cause I only ate the holes!

Would You Rather...

Would you rather be a tiger? Or would you be a bear?
Would you rather be an apple?   Or a freshly fallen pear?
Would you rather be a sports car? Or an eighteen wheel truck?
Would you rather be a long neck goose? Or would you be a duck?
Would you rather be the sunshine?   Or would you be the moon?
Would you rather write a book?   Or compose a happy tune?
Would you rather be a trumpet? Or would you be a drum?
Would you rather be a finger? Or would you be a thumb?
Would you rather be a mountain? Or would you be the sea?
Would you rather be an "A+?" Or settle for a "C?"
Would you rather be a pizza? Or a hot dog in a bun?
    I hope I got you thinking. I hope that you had fun.

Polite

If burping was considered nice,
If showering was rude,
If using hands was back in style
when slurping down your food...
If elbows on the table
Was just the thing to do,
To wipe your nose upon your sleeve,
No longer was taboo.
If...NOT saying please and thank you
Was considered quite all right
I think you may, I think you might,
Consider ME polite!

Talk

I hear the dogs bark in the yard.
I hear the purring cats.
I hear the chirping birdies sing.
I hear the squeaking rats.
The lions roar. The hippos burp.
The monkeys seem to screech.
The seals make some funny sounds
While lying on the beach.
I hear the piggy's grunt and snort.
I hear the mules braying.
These animals - they seem to talk.
I wonder what they're saying?

Rain

Rain can make the brown grass green.
    It makes the flowers bloom.
Just watch the trees and watch the weeds -
    they zoom, zoom, zoom, zoom, zoom!
Rain can cool a summer day.
    But, now it's rather tough.
It's rained and rained for two weeks straight.
    I think we've had enough!

Questions

Who? When?
Where? They ask.
Why? And then..How come?
It seems that asking questions,
Is, for kids, a rule of thumb.
They never seem to stop. I'm trying to stay calm.
When I finally think I've had enough,
    I yell - 'Go ask your mom!'

Jack & Jill

Jack and Jill went up the hill,
   to fetch a pail of water.
Jack - he was a neighbor boy.
   Jill - she is my daughter.
Jack fell down and broke his crown,
   and, sadly, he did die.
And, though it's sad, I have to say...
   ...I never liked the guy!

I know I had a question.
But, now I'm quite distraught.
I know I had a question?
But, it seems I've plum forgot!
?????

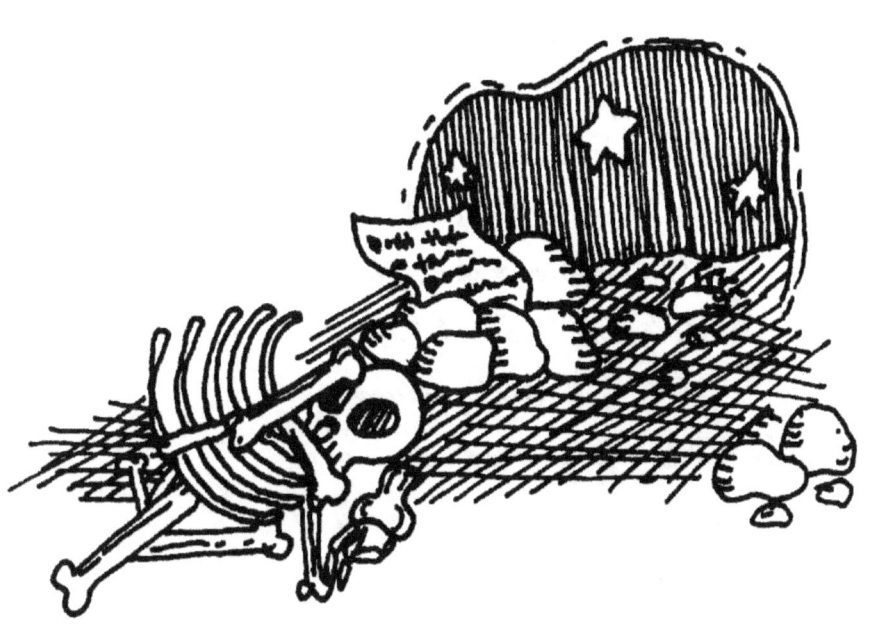

Tarantula

DON'T TICKLE A TARANTULA -
IT'S NOT THE THING TO DO.
RUN UNTIL YOUR LEGS GIVE OUT,
IF ONE COMES INTO VIEW.
DON'T PET HIS LITTLE WHISKERS,
DON'T PINCH HIS CUTE REAR-END.
NO MATTER WHAT YOU DO OR SAY,
HE'LL NEVER BE A FRIEND.
THESE WORDS WERE ON A LETTER,
I FOUND AMONG SOME STONES,
INSIDE A LITTLE CAVE,
BESIDE A PILE OF **BONES**.

Grandma's Gone

The good Lord took my Grandma.
    I'll miss her smiling face.
Her wholesome laugh that shook the ground,
    Is one you can't replace.
Her little notes and gifts she made,
    The way she made me laugh,
Are reasons why, I believe…
    She <u>**was**</u> the better half.
Yes…the good Lord took my Grandma.
    I cannot help but frown,
And, ask the Lord the question…
    "Why's <u>Grandpa</u> still around?!"

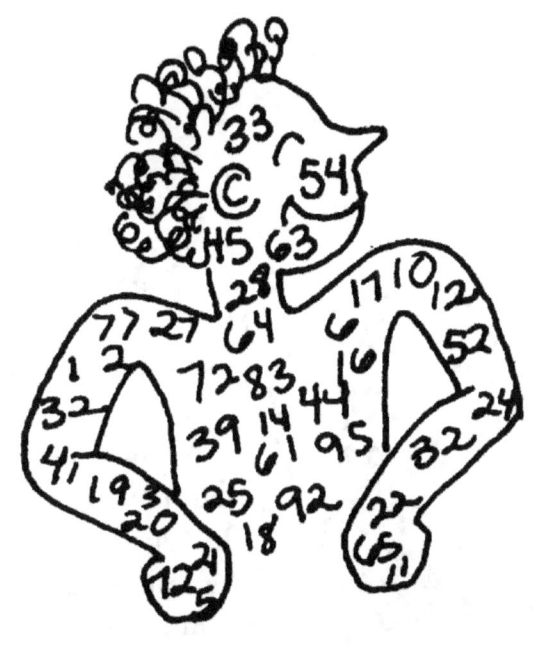

Brand New Marker

I found a brand new marker,
    took off my shirt and then...
Started writing numbers –
    all the way to 10!
I filled my arms and legs.
    My chest was covered too.
By the time I did my stomach,
    I was up to 92.
I put them on my hands.
    I put them on my feet.
There's numbers on my eyelids.
    There's numbers on my seat.
I'm covered head to toe –
    so Mom and Dad can see...
That if they are in need............
    ....they can **count** on me!

$$$$$$$$

My mother named me Penny
She named my brother Dime.
It's not that big of deal.
It's nowhere near a crime.
She named our kitty Quarter.
Our guinea pig is Nickel.
When naming family members,
my mother's rather fickle.
She calls my daddy "Dollar,"
instead of Jim or "Honey."
She thinks this is the only way
she'll ever have some money.

PYTHON

The python is an amazing snake.
And, I should know you see.
For wrapped around my skinny frame,
is a python, squeezing me!

Careful

*Be careful when you're passing gas.
Beware of wind direction.
Be sure to warn your friends because...
they might need nose protection.
Your smell can burn my eyes and nose.
It seems you are a pro.
But, consider what your friends will think
before you let one go.
Be careful when you're passing gas.
I hope you are aware...
that though you may be proud of it,
we wish you wouldn't share!*

SHOW ME

If you ask to see my dog,
    my skateboard, or my brother
or, want an introduction
    to my dad or to my mother,
I'll tell you it's no problem.
    It's an easy thing to do,
One by one or all at once –
    I'll bring them into view.
I'll show you my guitar.
    I'll share my favorite book.
You want to see my bedroom?
    Go ahead – take a look.
There aren't too many things
    I won't share or I won't show.
But, if you ask to see my birthmark –
    I'll kindly tell you "NO!"

Things

A beetle, a goldfish, a centipede, a snake -
these are creature I find by the lake.
A kitty, a goldfish, a lizard, a mouse -
these are pets we keep in our house.
Computers, rulers, pencils, and pens
teachers, principals, nurses and friends,
textbooks and desks, crayons and rules -
these are some things you will find in all schools.
Pots and pans, dishes and towels,
rakes and ladders, spades and trowels,
toothpaste and soap and shaving cream foam -
these are some things you find in a home.
Tires, wheels, a radio and more,
mirrors and windshield, mats on the floor,
Bumpers, lights, specks of old tar -
these are things you find on a car.
A watch, a shirt, pants and some skin,
brown hair, brown eyes, and most always a grin,
two hands, two feet, two elbows, two knees -
these are some things... that you find on me!

To the Teacher

I wish for you a year of smiles
For in your heart you know,
That you are touching children's lives
And, helping young minds grow.
I thank you now for all you'll do
For all the things you'll share
For daily doing things that show...
How much you truly care.

PLANS

I meant to paint the fence today,
   I meant to mow the lawn.
I meant to get a haircut,
   and, call my brother, Jon.
I meant to wash the car today,
   I meant to wash my clothes.
What happened to my lofty plans?
.......who knows?!

Be Nice

Here's a bit of wisdom.
Read it more than once or twice.
It's nice to be important...
But, more important to be nice!

THE SCARE

I WENT INSIDE THE HAUNTED HOUSE.
I KNEW WITHOUT A DOUBT,
IT WOULDN'T BE TOO LONG AT ALL,
'TILL I WAS WANTING OUT!
I SAW THE STICKY SPIDER WEBS.
I SAW THE SCARY GHOSTS.
I SAW THE WITCHES' PEA-GREEN SOUP;
IT MADE ME SICK - ALMOST.
BUT, WHEN YOU CAME BEHIND ME,
AND, SHOUTED IN MY EAR,
I COULDN'T HELP WHAT I DID NEXT,
FOR, I WAS FILLED WITH FEAR.
THAT'S WHY YOU HAVE A BLOODY NOSE,
AND ONE SORE, TENDER SHIN.
MY ADVICE...JUST THINK TWICE,
BEFORE YOU SCARE AGAIN!

I Can?

I can drive the fastest car
and fly the fastest plane.
I can stop a locomotive train
and stop a hurricane.
I can wrestle with the biggest beast
and win most ANY fight.
My friends, they say,
it can't be done.
You know,.....
I think they're right!

I FEEL LIKE PLAYING IN MUD

I feel like playing in mud today.
I feel like mixing the dirt,
With water and sand and sticks and leaves —
who cares if it gets on my shirt.
I feel like playing in mud today.
I'll going to make mud pies and cakes.
I'll fashion some into a bread loaf.
I'll mold some into a steak.
I'll paint my walls and my windows.
I'll try to paint the whole town.
I'll cover our car and van,
in a beautiful shade of brown.
I feel like playing in mud today.
I'll invite my family and friends.
We'll have the grandest mud party.
We'll be covered in dirt when it ends.
I feel like playing in mud today.
Come join us and then you will see,
That this is the wish for my birthday
'cuz today I turn...43!

My Pet Hen

The hen I have is jitterish,
    She jumps at sudden sounds.
When thunder roars she's sure to run
    'round and 'round and 'round.
She's full of fear. She's full of fright.
    She's fully panic stricken.
I guess that you would have to say
    I have a "chicken" chicken!

Happy Hydrant

I'm a happy fire hydrant
But, dogs just drive me crazy.
They think I am a rosebush'
or a fir tree or, a daisy.
I'm a happy fire hydrant.
Or, at least I used to be.
Until the dogs came walking by
  and tried to water me!

Get Down

Who needs a chair?
Who needs a table?
Get down on the floor.
It's much more stable.
Nothing to wobble.
Nothing to tip.
Nothing to stain.
Nothing to chip.
So, here's my advice –
it's safe and it's sound.
Throw furniture out
and live on the ground!

PORCUPINE

While camping in the summertime,
I sat upon a porcupine.
I looked at him, he looked at me.
He said, "Would you please pardon me?"
And, then he played a clarinet.
Now, THAT'S a day I won't forget!

Rude

Burping isn't really bad.
    Farting's not a crime.
But, think about the PLACE it's done,
    and think about the TIME.
Don't do them in a church or school
    where one might hear or smell -
these natural body functions
    We all know, oh, SO well.
But, **IF** the room is empty,
    No one is around...
BURP to make the walls shake!
    FART to move the ground!

Cannot Sleep

I cannot get to sleep tonight.
I cannot close my eyes.
I cannot get relaxed at all.
It comes as no surprise.
It's not because I'm hungry.
But, what it is I dread -
the covers that have
   kept me warm...
Are... on YOUR side of the bed!
So, now I lay here freezing.
Warmth is what I lack.
You've taken all the covers.
Please...just give them back!

Laugh

I laughed until my eyes were red.
I laughed until I cried.
I laughed so hard, I thought I'd split,
from side to aching side.
I laughed so hard I rolled and rolled.
I even did a dance.
I should have stopped right then and there,
'cause next .....I wet my pants!

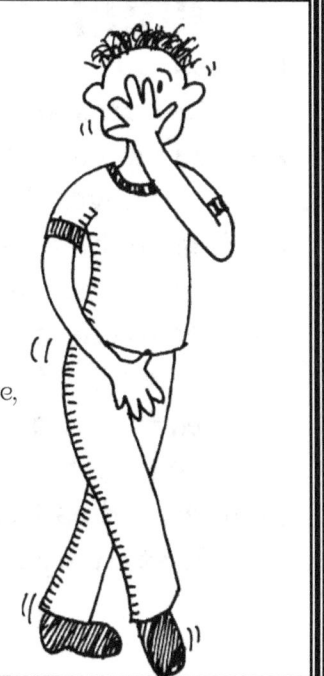

DOGS

55 million dogs in this land.
    55 million, they say.
55 million dogs in this land
    that run and bark and play.
They're man's best friend (and women's too!).
    They love both girls and boys.
They don't need much - a hug or two
    and food, water, and toys.
Yes, 55 million dogs it said.
    I read it on a sign.
55 million dogs in this land....
    NOT **ONE** OF THEM IS MINE!
Mom...can I pleeeeaaase get a dog?

DOG GONE

My doggy is a little weird.
    He barks at bees and flies.
He barks at cars and kids on bikes,
    whenever they go by.
He digs big holes in our backyard
    and, in our neighbor's, too.
He likes to chew on all our chairs;
    He's ruined quite a few!
He likes to chase my best friend's dad.
    He likes to chase his tail.
He doesn't do a thing I say.
    That's why my dog's for sale.

DOG DECISIONS

Should I jump upon the couch?
Should I chew upon the chair?
Should I lick my master's feet?
Should I shed a little hair?
Do I want to dig a big hole?
Do I even want to try?
Do I want to have my food today,
Canned, or... maybe... dry?
Do I want to chase a car,
Or sniff a new found log?
I think there's quite a few,
Decisions for a dog.

CATS

OK...Who drooled on my pillow?
    Who spilled the juice? Who licked the Jello-O?
Who clawed the couch? Who killed the rats?
    There's no doubt in my mind...it had to be cats!
Who sleeps on the counters? Who sleeps in the chair?
    Who sleeps all day? Which hardly seems fair.
Who leaves their fur, on coats and on hats?
    Yes, it's true, it's those darn cats!
Who stretches at length? Who rolls on their back?
    Who's a finicky eater, but is still getting fat?!
Who makes me laugh, until I'm quite giddy?
    You've guessed it again. It's my silly kitty!
Who catches snakes? Who chases squirrels?
    Who catches the attention of all of the girls?
Who catches mice, birds and some gnats?
    That's right, my friends...it's those crazy cats!
Whose tail is always moving? Whose paws knead the rug?
    Whose first to let you know, that they need a hug?
Whose fur makes my nose itch? Whose dander makes me zitty?
    That's right, folks...it's my darling kitty!

A cat in the home,
can be a frustrating pet,
and yet,
if you met
my pet
I bet
you'd get
one too!

Smart Dog

I love my little beagle dog.
    He couldn't be much cuter.
And, now he'll be a smarter dog,
    'cause, today he's getting tutored!
(What mommy? It's not tutored? Well...what's THAT mean?)

Snake

A snake can slither slowly.
A snake can slither fast.
The way they creep upon the ground,
is really unsurpassed.
So, in my daddy's garden
I get down on the ground.
I pretend I am a python
and move without a sound.
I scrape my stomach on a rock.
I squish a slug or two.
My elbow, in the morning,
will be red, and black, and blue!
My backbone's getting out of joint.
It feels like it might break.
I think I've learned a lesson....
I couldn't be a snake!

HORSES

It's fun to ride, and ride all day
upon a nice tall horse.
But, when I'm done - I want no more.
(My seat is sore, of course!)

WALRUS

I MET A WALRUS, AND I SAID,
"YOU SURE DO HAVE BUCK TEETH!"
NOW, HE IS UP ON TOP OF ME.
AND I, AM UNDERNEATH!

Parakeet

My parakeet is full of pep.
   She's nowhere near a slacker.
She always talks,
   but, mostly says,
   "Polly wants a cracker!"
But, when you go to pet my bird,
I'll warn you - please don't linger.
It just might be the day, today
   .....that Polly wants a finger!

PET PROBLEMS

If a dog gets a booger, or a cat, a runny nose,
   I know of their solution. I'll tell you...here goes:
They can't quite wipe that nose of theirs.
   They can't quite seem to pick it.
But, they have a long wet willing tongue,
   So....they lick it, lick it, lick it!

New Kitten

I just got a new little kitten.
    Although he's furry and cute,
His behavior is more than peculiar.
    His actions are less than astute.
At night when our family is sleeping –
    it's quiet and peaceful and dark –
when he hears the slightest of sounds,
    he'll run to the door and he'll bark!
And, when I get out of the shower,
    he'll run up and jump on my towel.
He'll tug and he'll pull and he'll shake.
    He'll huff and he'll puff and he'll growl.
In the morning he'll bring me my slippers.
    The paper? He'll bring it in, too.
He's buried some bones in my garden.
    What will this cat not do?
He's learned how to fetch and roll over.
    He's learned how to beg and play dead.
I thought I had asked for a kitten
    ...they gave me a puppy instead.

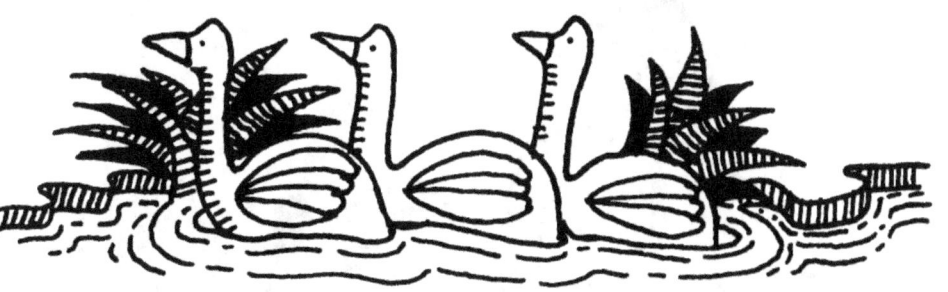

A Gaggle of Geese

It's a brood of young birds, and a gaggle of geese.
I'll tell you some more, if you just say *"pleese"*.
a herd of cattle, a drift of hogs,
a gang of elk, a kennel of dogs,
a pride of lions, a shoal of whales,
a nest of rabbits, a bevy of quails,
A flock of swans, a hive of bees,
a school of fish, that live in the seas,
A drove of sheep, a sloth of bears,
a swarm of insects…could get in you hair.
A watch of nightingales, a sounder of wild hogs,
a colony of ants, that live in the logs,
A trip of seal, a herd of deer,
these rhymes are getting harder… I fear.
So, remember the names of animals in groups,
And, for now I'll say…so long, troops!

HORSE

I rode the horse all day today.
    I'm glad that it was sunny.
But, I think I rode a tad too long,
    'Cause now I'm walking funny!
My legs look like a horseshoe!
    My walk has quite a sway!
Do I want to ride again?
    Right now my answer's..... neigh!

SPIDER

There's a spider in my hat.
Can you imagine that?
I'm such a fraidy cat,
when there's a spider in my hat.
There's a spider in my hat.
I throw it in a vat.
I crank the thermostat.
He got out! That dirty rat!
There's a spider on the mat.
I think I'll squish him flat.
Gosh, he sure is fat.
I step on him and....SPLAT!
And that...is that!

The Chicken and the Human

"I'm a human," said the chicken.
"I'm afraid of many things;
I'm afraid of snakes and spiders
And anything that stings."
"I'm a human," said the chicken.
"I hardly think it's fair.
I shake at scary movies
I tremble at a dare.
I do not like dark places,
I shiver when there's thunder.
If I hear an owl hoot,
The covers I get under."
"I'm a human," said the chicken.
"It's a fact I don't enjoy."
"I'm a human," said the chicken.
"I'm a chicken," ...said the boy.

BETTER PETS

*If I could play, for just awhile,
with a big green crocodile
I'd scratch his back, I'd rub his head.
I'd scrub his teeth, I'd make his bed.
Then, there's times, I feel must,
ride a hippopotamus,
I'd be quite glad, to say the least
to ride upon a hippo beast.
And, if I could, do a stunt
up upon an elephant,
I'd wash his trunk and clean his ears.
That would get some smiles and cheers.
But, if I could, wish some more,
I'd ride upon a dinosaur.
I'd be so high, up off the ground,
I wish those things were still around!
But, all I have is my kitty cat,
and he's a little too lazy, and a little too fat.
Bu,t I love him, and he loves me,
and that's the way, it's supposed to be.*

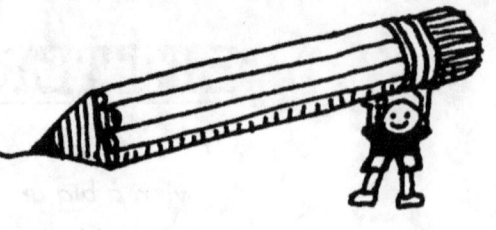

My Way

I talk the way I want to talk.
    I walk the way I please.
I live the way I want to live.
    I'm really quite at ease.
I write the way I want to write.
    I choose the way I sit.
I thought I'd share these thoughts with you,
    so....this is what I writ.

Too Much

My sister ate a pickle,
    ate a penguin, drank a pop.
        Ate a lamb, ate a lizard,
            ate a yellow lollipop.
                Ate a sow, ate a cow;
                    I'm sure that must have filled her.
                    Ate a quail, then a whale;
                    THAT'S...what finally...
                        killed her.

DON'T BE AFRAID

Don't be afraid, to try a new sport -
you just might find that you like it!
Don't be afraid, to put on your boots
and find a mountain and hike it!
Don't be afraid, to read a hard book -
it's good to challenge the mind.
Don't be afraid, to search for the truth -
for peace and joy you might find.
Don't be afraid, to make a new friend -
the truth is, you can't have too many.
Don't be afraid, to save what you earn -
just start by saving a penny!
Don't be afraid, if you do something good,
to jump and holler and hoot!
And, don't be afraid, to go out on a limb,
'Cause at the end of a limb........is the fruit

Good Learners

Good learners are hard working -
   they never seem to end.
Good learners are creative -
   they imagine and pretend.
They're also empathetic -
   they feel what others feel.
They're resourceful, so they research,
   with a much determined zeal.
And when it comes to risks,
   they're not afraid at all.
For, they know they can bounce back,
   from a set-back, or a fall.
And, they're always kind and thoughtful,
   they think of others first.
And, in the skills of scheduling,
   they really are well versed.
These traits are quite impressive
   but, they're really nothing new.
So, **IF** you learn and practice,
   they can be a part of **YOU**!

No Artist

I tried to draw my brother Jon –
it looked more like an ape.
I tried to build a paper plane –
I used a ton of tape.
I tried my hand at sculpturing.
I tried my best to paint.
Of all the things I know I am,
An artist I just ain't!

Hair

My hair has always been a chore.
    It's oily, flat, and straight.
It's hard to get my friends to say,
    "Boy, your hair looks great!"
But, now it seems I'm going bald.
    It seems it is my fate.
As time goes on, it seems to me...
    There's little left to hate!

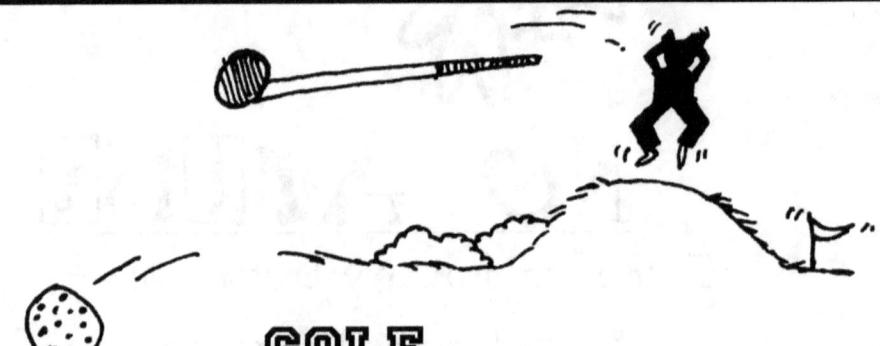

GOLF

My brother is a golf nut.
    and so he thought one day.
He'd take me to the golf course
    and show me how to play.
I've practiced and I've practiced.
    But, I need to practice more.
For every time I hit the ball,
    I'm always yelling ....FORE!

Wish

Someone has to wash the clothes
and wash the car and dishes.
Someone has to feed the dog
and feed the cat and fishes.
Someone has to mow the lawn,
and pull up all the weeds.
There are many, many jobs to do.
There are many, many needs.
Someone has to do the work,
But, here's my simple plea;
I wish, I wish, I wish, I wish
...I wish it wasn't ME!

Wedgy

I gave a wedgy
to my friend.
He gave one back to me.
We're walking kind of funny now.
Just try it
...you will see!

Bath

I've been sitting in this bathtub
Since the 23rd of June.
It's mid July and my oh my!
I look just like a prune!
It's August now and, holy cow,
My body makes me wince!
I took that one long bath that day
.....I've been wrinkled ever since!

Sweet Lesson

I ate a bunch of candy
and, boy, it made me sick!
I had to find a bathroom
and, I had to find it quick!
I learned a couple lessons.
Just listen, here they are....
Pace yourself on suckers.
 Don't overdue... on candy bars!

Move It!

I had to move the fridge today.
    For help, I asked my dad.
We worked so hard, our muscles ached.
    We started to get mad.
With him in front and me in back,
    We could not figure why...
This fridge, it didn't move an inch.
        Oh...Dad...you're pushing?!   So am I!

Back to Bed

I woke up with a cold today,
Then, at the breakfast table,
I poured a bowl of soapy suds.
I somehow missed the label.
I stepped upon a skateboard,
While walking to the bus.
I left my homework home today;
My teacher made a fuss.
At lunch I ate a sandwich,
That was made from moldy bread.
I said out loud, in fact I screamed....
"I should have stayed in BED!"

HUGS

A hug's a perfect gift – one size fits big and small
and if someone does return it – no one minds at all.
A hug can be a gift - for a birthday celebration,
for Christmas or Thanksgiving – or any nice occasion.
A hug can be quite short – then, again, it can be long.
You can give them when you're tired – or when you're feeling strong.
They're great when someone's happy - they help when someone's sad.
They're a little hard to give - when someone's feeling mad.
They show that you are friendly - they show that you do care.
So, give them out at home - or give them anywhere.
If you give or if you get - you both will feel quite good.
If you haven't ever tried this - I really think you should.
Yes, a hug's a perfect gift – and best of all they're fun
      and if you're not too busy - I'd like to give you one!

Pumpkin Time

Three plump and bright orange pumpkins -
we'll carve them all tonight.
One face happy, one face sad,
one face full of fright!
We get out all the carving knives,
and then we place our bets.
We always see how long it takes,
'till Daddy breaks a sweat!
We watch him as he shapes the face.
We watch him do his stuff.
He wipes his brow, he's working hard.
We hear him huff and puff!
When Daddy gets the last one done,
"Hooray!" is what we shout.
But, Daddy quickly finds the couch,
'Cause Daddy's tuckered out!

Christmas Wish

We got out all our Christmas stuff,
 the lights and plastic tree.
We put it up, with sweat and pride,
 for everyone to see.
Our house, it looked the very best.
 But, then I gave a sigh.
Our house, it looked the very best....
 and here it is...JULY!

****

The Season

A very Merry Christmas
 is what I wish for you.
A time to give some gifts
 and maybe get a few!
A time for love and kindness.
 A time for peace and joy.
A time for hope and laughter,
 For every girl and boy.
A time for new beginning
 A time for good old friends.
This season comes so quickly,
 And quickly it will end.

ADVICE FOR SANTA

Santa's in the chimney,
   but, it's not a pretty sight.
It's always been a snug fit
   but, now it's just plain tight!
With an ever growing belly,
   it seems it was his fate
That sooner, more than later,
   he'd HAVE to loose some

...weight!

Holiday News

Kwanza is from Africa.
   Hanakah, from Jews.
Christmas is from Christian faith.
   But, here's some breaking news;
I've made up a new holiday.
   You shouldn't make a fuss.
'Cause I've named this brand new holiday,
Kwana-Hana-Mas!

'Tis the Season

Silent night?! Oh yeah....right!
The kids are more than loud.
How can a two-kid family,
sound like a football crowd?
They're swinging from the ceiling!
They're bouncing off the walls!
My head is near exploding.
I need some Tylenol!
About right now my patience,
is really wearing thin.
It's easy to conclude,
It's Christmas time again!

THE CHRISTMAS TREE

*The young noble fir,
tried hard to look good.
He'd like to be chosen.
He'd like that. He would.
Chosen to be,
that one special tree,
Donned for Christmas,
for all eyes to see.
And, chosen he was.
They sawed him right down.
They snipped and they clipped.
He tried not to frown.
And, though he looked pretty,
in deed quite fantastic,
he wished they had picked,
a tree...made of plastic.*

Decorating

We gathered 'round,
to trim the tree.
"I get the top!"
I yelled with glee.
The lights went on,
the tinsel, too.
And, ornaments,
both old and new.
Then at last,
the time had come
To top the tree,
it should be fun.
But, something happened.
Something bad.
It made me angry.
It made me sad.
While standing on
the shaky ladder,
I tipped the tree
and things did shatter.
My family looked at me
and, then...
I said, "Oh well...
Let's start again!"

EARLY GIFT

T'was the night before Christmas,
and all through our home
the kids were all screaming,
while the wife's on the phone.
The dog's outside barking,
the cat claws the couch.
I think for this Christmas,
I'll be the grouch!
Then, slowly, but surely,
the commotion did settle,
The whistling stopped,
from our old tea pot kettle.
A magical spell
had encompassed our dwelling.
There were smiles on the faces –
no frowning or yelling.
The family has gathered,
all in one room.
Their faces all shining,
like a bride and her groom.
So, what is this secret?
Just join us, you'll see.
Our early Christmas present….
a brand new TV!

Slow Going

I have a pounding headache.
    It makes it hard to think.
In my finger there's a splinter.
    In my neck there is a kink.
My bottom has a big bruise.
    I fell and scraped my knee.
I hit my funny bone and then...
    I sat upon a bee!
A piece of dust flew in my eye.
    I also stubbed my toe.
I've got a splitting side ache.
    That's why I'm moving slow!

VOMIT

My brother says it's quite routine,
That vomit's, mostly yellow-green.
He says it tastes quite bitter and,
It helps to eat some food that's bland.
Out your mouth and out your nose,
Food that's halfway decomposed.
He says it comes both thin and thick.

"Stop!", I say... "I'm getting sick!"

RULES

Be happy and be kind.
    Be helpful with a smile.
If you argue, if you quarrel,
    Be quick to reconcile.
Be respectful. Be polite.
    Please....don't act like fools.
Listen close and learn a lot.
    Class, these are the rules.
        Now if you can't agree,
        If you whine
          or, if you pout
            .....GET OUT!

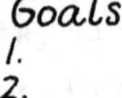

PLAN to PLAN

If you plan to finish High School
    and graduate from college,
If you plan to read a thousand books
    and fill your head with knowledge,
If you plan to learn all through your life
    and die a wise old man,
There's something that you ought to know...
    you'd better learn to plan!

Cloud 9

She's dancing on a rainbow,
She's dancing on a cloud.
She dances round and round the room,
She starts to sing out loud.
She's acting like a beauty queen,
She's acting like a clown.
Then I hear the teacher say...
"PLEASE...would you sit down?!"

DONNY'S DESK

Donny's desk is messy - it's sort of smelly, too.
Whenever I pass by it, I have to say, P-U!
The books are getting moldy, as are his paints and glue.
And, stuffed inside this little desk, is one old rotting shoe!
It's home to candy wrappers, some crickets and a mouse.
This desk, it is a messy desk, but, you should see
.....his HOUSE!

TEACHER'S LAST LECTURE

You never got your homework done.
   You daydreamed half the day.
You didn't care about the rules,
   Or, what I had to say.
Your mouth, you couldn't seem to shut.
   You couldn't find your seat.
To my dismay, I have to say...
   This grade - you will repeat!

Crisis In Class

There's a booger on my finger, and I can't get it off!
    It's a little bit too gooey, it's a little bit too soft.
Now, what should I do, since I'm sitting here in class?
    I guess it could be worse, I could have had some gas.
And, gas can make noise, and sometimes even linger.
    But, right now the problem is, this booger on my finger!
My nose was really itchy, I just really had to pick-it.
    It wasn't much a problem, until I tried to flick-it!
At first it left my finger, then...'bout an inch or so away,
    it quickly snapped on back, and there it seems to stay!
They're usually not so gooey, but, this one is just like glue.
    And, I feel I know my boogers, I've examined quite a few!
Oh, now I know the trick, I learned it oh, so young.
    When I see that no one's looking, I grab it with my tongue!
        Yum Yum!

Love & Lies

I love to do my homework.
    I love to clean my room.
I love to go out in the garage,
    and sweep it with a broom.
I love to take the garbage out.
    I love to wash and dry.
I bet you've figured out by now
    .....I also love to lie!

Help?

Here I sit in school,
   my stomach in a knot.
What was it that the teacher said?
   What was it that she taught?
I'm so afraid to ask her.
   In fact, I'm scared to death.
I know that she will help me.
   But, BOY
      ...she has bad breath!

Homework

Please help me with my homework.
   Please help me right away.
   In fact..... just do it for me,
   So I can go and play!

The Greatest Fault

Some people have trouble doing math in their head.
    Others don't know the words they've just read.
Some find it hard - to write or to spell.
    Others can't seem ...to speak very well.
Some click their fork on their teeth when they eat.
    Some belch out loud and, are never discreet.
Some have big noses. Some have big ears.
    Some are compelled ...to have many fears.
Some suck their thumbs. Some bite their nails.
    Some are quite hyper.   Some are like snails.
We all have our faults, probably more than just ONE.
    But, the greatest of faults...is to be conscious
                            .....of none!

No Hair

There's nothing on my head to comb.
    There's not a single hair.
It fills me with great sadness.
    It fills me with despair.
But, you shouldn't be surprised.
    You shouldn't be appalled.
To find another eagle....
    ...that's bald.

GERMS

We complain of being sick.
We despise those pesky germs.
But, aren't you glad they're not...
The size of pachyderms!

success

Some want to grow up, and write many books.
Some, plan to be a chef or a cook.
While others may dream, of teaching young minds,
Some dream of cars, and brand new designs.
Some want to build. Some want to dance.
Some want to study, creatures or plants.
Some will be lawyers, and some will save lives.
Some will be mothers when babies arrive.
Now, some say success, is reaching a goal.
Dreaming a dream, and making it so.
But, one thing is true, I just have to say.
Tomorrow's success, begins....TODAY!

DIET

If eating crocodile eyes
With beets and leeks and yams,
Or, rattlesnakes or monkey brains
Or slimy, smelly clams,
You might just think it has to be
the most repulsive dinner.
But, think it through and you will see
.....at least you're getting thinner!

LISTEN

Six feet underground I am,
I wish it was a trick!
And, I wish you would have listened
.....'Cause I told you I was sick!

ZUKES

I planted ten zucchini seeds.
And, by the way they grew,
I knew I'd get zucchinis and,
I think more than a few.
And, sure enough, you can't believe
the crop I grew this year!
We picked them all but, when we did,
they seemed to reappear!
I thought I'd do a neighbor thing
and give a few away.
O,r better yet, just pick a bunch,
and put them on display.
I put some on a wooden chair,
and placed them by the street
In hopes a friend would see them there,
and take them home to eat.
I placed a sign beside them all
Its only word was "FREE."
How long before they'd all be gone?
I'd have to wait and see.
The next day when I came to check,
I couldn't help but stare.
The zukes, it seemed, had not been touched,
But, missing.....was my chair!

Homonym Scholar

I heard a herd of cows, that were walking in the sun.
Then a ewe heard you, and started to run.
The horse was hoarse, and couldn't quite neigh.
The new gnu knew you, and wanted to play.
The bare bear was embarrassed and started to blush.
And the flea did flee, in an incredible rush.
The boar tried to bore a hole in the wall,
as the birds with the flu, that flew...did fall.
Now, the moose put on mousse – for his hair was quite long,
While the hair on the hare was short, stiff, and strong.
The mussels with muscles went to the best spot,
While the three-toed toad, was towed off the lot.
Then, the fowl called foul, when playing a game.
And the deer, my dear friends, all did the same.
This poem is near over, but don't you dare holler.
For now you can say, "I'm a HOMONYM scholar!"

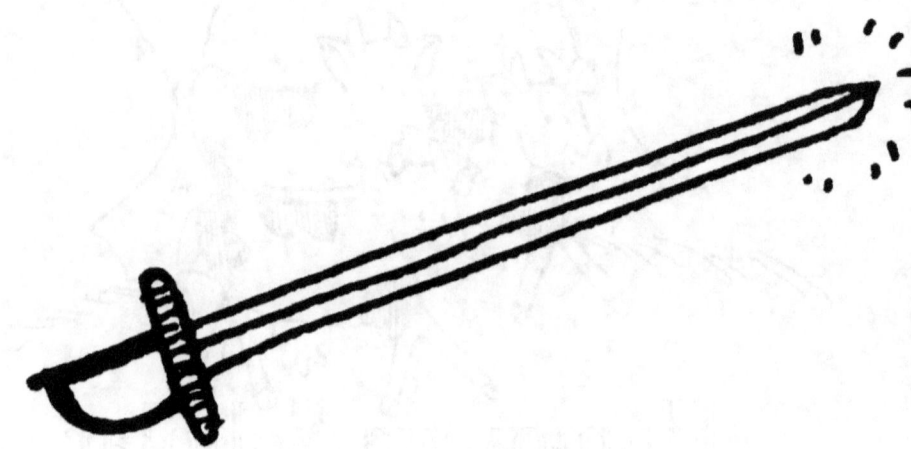

Sword Swallower

I saw a man
put down his throat
a sword 'bout 10 feet long.
He tried to talk.
He tried to yell.
He tried to sing a song.
But, all I heard,
it sounded like,
a long and painful wail.
For, that sword had slipped,
and now he had,
A shiny, pointy... tail!

Dare Devil

My brother wants to bungee jump. He says that I should, too.
   He wants to buy a sailboat, and sail the ocean blue.
He wants to ride a wild bull and drive a racing car.
   He says it would be loads of fun. I say it sounds bazaar.
He says he wants to dive the cliffs - the ones in Mexico.
   He says he wants to scuba dive. I say, 'Well, I don't know."
He wants to jump from a plane! I think that is the WORST!
He looks at me. I finally say, "OK, ...but, you go first!"

ROOM GLOOM

I get all hot and start to sweat.
My tummy starts to ache.
My head....it starts to spin around.
My legs begin to shake.
My kidneys hurt. My heart does, too.
I'm filled with doom and gloom,
   When Mommy says, "It's time now, Son....
     ...to go and clean your room!"

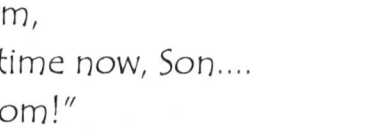

MAGIC BRO

My brother's a magician.
He did the greatest trick.
My mother was completely shocked.
It almost made her sick.
He crawled into the lion cage.
I admit it's kind of weird.
But, he waved his magic wand around,
and POOF, he disappeared!
The lion smacked his lips and grinned,
as if he'd had a snack.
Hmmm. I wonder if my brother,
can use his magic.... to come back?

NOT-SO-FUNNY BONE

Today I hit my funny bone.
It nearly made me cry.
The funny bone? Who named it that?
I cannot figure why.
For, as I rub my aching arm,
while lying on this couch,
The only words that come to me
are ouch, ouch, ouch, ouch, OUCH!

Secret

Don't let your parents know this.
Do you promise? Cross your heart?
I heard it from my brother.
And, my brother's **very** smart!
I know where babies come from.
The secret baby store!
Don't let your parents know this!
They might go get some more!
And, if my mommy asks me,
I'll be strong. I will resist her.
'Cause, if I let her know ....
She might bring home a sister!

DINNER JOKE

My mom was fixing dinner. I asked her what it was.
She said it was raw eel, stuffed with belly button fuzz.
With craw dads as a side dish. For dessert, cold artichoke.
Mom, I'm really hungry! This better be a joke!

Mealtime

I've had this meal a thousand times,
I've seen it all before.
If I could... have my way,
I'd throw it out the door.
I'd hop into the family car
I feel I'm in the mood,
To drive around and find a place
Where we can get fast food.
But, here I sit with Mom and Dad,
They're grumbling and they're staring.
My feeling is tonight they'll be
...WAY too overbearing!
I've had this meal a thousand times.
It feels like it's a crime.
But, to please my mom and dad
.....I'll have it ONE more time.

Dad's Beard

I thought I saw
    a pair of eyes,
In daddy's
    dark brown beard.
It looked a little creepy and
    it looked a little weird.
But, the eyes,
    they were my sister Sue's.
And, though I may be wrong,
    I think my daddy's
dark brown beard,
    is just a bit too long!

Mom's Working

My mother started working.
  Tonigh,t she's working late.
At first I thought it terrible.
  But, now I think it's great.
Yes, having mommy work tonight,
  is really not that bad.
'Cause it's sure to guarantee,
  another PIZZA night with Dad!

Lollipop

I dropped my lollipop today.
It made my body pucker.
'Cause...it's not an easy task...
To lick a fuzzy sucker!

ALLOWANCE

I worked on all my chores this week.
   And, so I think it's fair,
To get a small allowance,
   Which, for me, has been quite rare.
So, I gather up the nerve to ask
   My parents what they think.
They say they're quite impressed with me,
   In fact, they're tickled pink.
They gave me an allowance but,
   I had to intervene,
To thank them for the money but,
   I wanted some that's green!

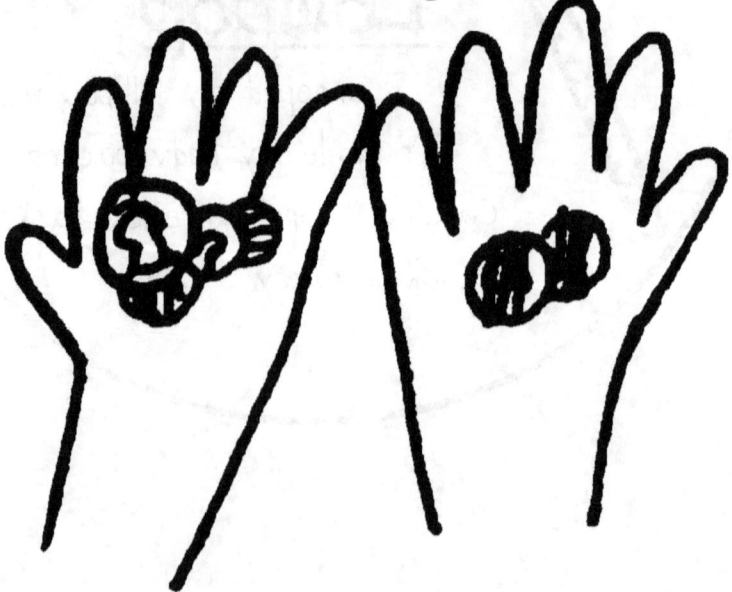

STILL ME?

If I could change my brown eyes,
if I could change my skin,
If I could gain a few more pounds,
instead of being thin,
If I could change my teeth,
and make them pearly white,
And, make them line up straight,
without an overbite,
If I could change my shoe size,
and improve my sense of sight,
Would it make a bit of difference,
if I gained a foot in height?
I would like to make these changes,
just so I could see
If I'd be someone else…
or….. if I would still be me.

TRY

I'm not sure I know how to do this.
    I'm not sure I can do this just right.
I don't want to sound pessimistic.
    And, I'm sure that I don't want to fight.
I'm not sure I know how to do this.
    It seems like an awfully hard task.
I'm not sure I know how to do this.
    It probably wouldn't hurt, if I'd ask.
I'm just a little bit worried.
    I don't want to make a mistake.
I'm thinking about all the problems,
    And, what a big mess I could make.
Yes, I'm not sure I know how to do this.
    I'm almost ready to cry.
I'm not sure I know how to do this.
    But, I guess I won't know, 'till I try!

Listen!

If you pick your nose, my mommy says,
Your finger will fall off.
Does not! - I scoff.
If you never change your underwear,
Your bladder will explode.
Not mine...I crowed!
If you never wash behind your ears,
You will lose your sense of hearing!
Reeeeeally?!   I said jeering!
Car keys, you will never get.
If you just can't take our hints.
I've listened ever since!

Step on a Crack....

You see the cracks upon the ground,
you see the jagged lines.
You think about the things you've learned,
from all those silly rhymes.
And, so you hop and skip and jump,
you're careful and discreet.
You know that cracks in concrete,
should never touch your feet!
But, what about the crack of dawn?
Should I avoid that too?
A cracking whip I will avoid,
I'm sure that you will too!
But, what if I should... crack a smile?
Or, maybe, crack a joke?
Would this break dear old mother's back?
Or, maybe make her croak?
And, what if I should crack a book?
Or, maybe crack some corn?
If I should crack my neighbor's safe,
I'm sure they'd be forlorn.
A wise-crack can evoke a smile,
and crack me up, and yet...
My voice cracks when I'm singing,
and that kind of makes me sweat!
Now, you might say I'm a crack-pot.
But, I'm not...so just relax.
So, here's a final warning....
Don't ever ....step on cracks!

Morning Chore

I got up in the morning,
I was half asleep and groggy.
But, I had to do my chores,
one, was feed the doggy.
But, somewhere in the process,
I mixed our two bowls up.
He seemed to like *his* breakfast,
as for me...I threw mine up!

Telephone Moan

In a voice both deep and raspy,
That rattles with loose phlegm,
I hear my daddy saying...
"Are you on the phone.....again?!"

Stone Soup

Once I read a story,
"Stone Soup," I do recall.
The soup was filled with flavor.
But, no cholesterol.
I made up my own batch.
I added quartz... and granite, too.
A little salt and pepper,
And, onions? Just a few.
I knew the stones were hard;
That's why I had to soak 'em.
I ate the soup today.
My teeth? I think I broke 'em!

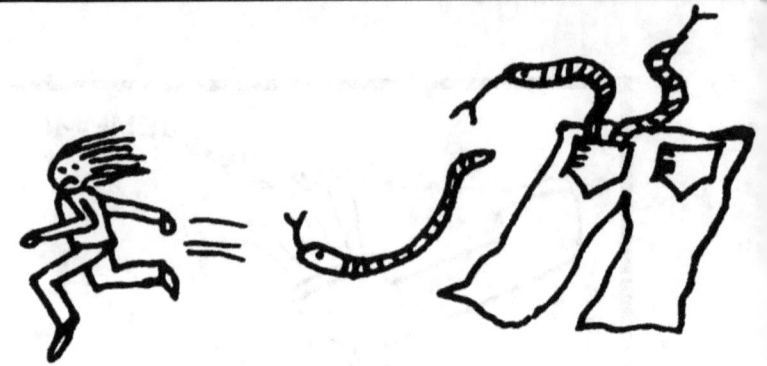

No Twin

Ants in my pants, dirt on my shirt,
  rocks in my socks, sure do hurt!
Snakes in my pockets. Scrapes on my skin.
  Mommy's sure glad.... I don't have a twin!

Diner Dilemma

Salad? - I don't think so.
Turnips? - None for me.
    Cauliflower, steamed or raw...
        I don't want to see!
        Broccoli? – No, thank you.
          Radishes? - Please, no.
            Liver and fried onions
              .....I think I need to go.

YUCK

BROCCOLI

My mommy's fixing broccoli.
 She just loves that color green.
But, forcing me to eat the stuff,
 is down right, plain ole mean!
She says it helps the body grow.
 She says it's healthy stuff.
But, chewing dark green broccoli,
 for me, is rather tough!
She says it makes for healthy skin.
 It could even bring good luck.
But, my ONLY word for broccoli..
.you know it...it's **YUCK!**

GREEN BANANAS

I like them green bananas.
    I like those unripe pears.
I eat them everyday for lunch.
    I always get some stares.
My uncle says they'll make me strong,
    and make my hair grow thick.
And...I'd like them even better if
    .....they didn't make me sick!

Sneezy

It's going to be a sneezy day.
    It's windy, warm and sunny.
While my sneezing might amuse my friends,
    To me it's just not funny!
Sneezing makes my eyes get red.
    It makes my stomach weak.
It makes my nose run all day long.
    It makes my bladder leak.
The reasons why I hate to sneeze,
    are more than just a few.
But, here is what I hate the most
    ...Achoo! Achoo! Achooooooo!

SICK

I threw up in the morning.
It made me feel much better.
My sister wants to see it.
I decide that I should let her.
We see a piece of popcorn.
We see some salad, too.
And, there's some hunks of hamburger
mixed in this vomit stew.
And, there's some chunks of chicken.
We count them, there are ten.
Oooooh, look out little sister,
I think I'm sick again!

Hungry

I'm so hungry that my vision's blurred,
I need some quick nutrition.
Please, find some food for me to eat
THIS ...is my petition.
I hear my stomach growling,
My taste buds are in need.
My body parts are screaming
"It's us you need to feed!"
I'm so hungry that I just might faint
Or worse, I just might die.
I need some tasty sustenance
Like ice cream, cake, or pie.
I'm so hungry that my knees are weak
So hungry that it hurts.
I'm ready to start eating now.
May I start with....the desserts?

Room Clean

To clean my room, you need a broom
You need a shovel, too.
I might suggest, it might be best
To bring a clean up crew.
And, with this task, I just might ask
For you to keep a smile.
To see the floor, and so much more,
It just might take awhile.
So, thank you Mom, please stay calm
I hope you just might see
As you clean today, I've got to say
I'm glad it's you, not me!

The Chase

I found a snake
   out in the grass -
      he turned and slithered on.
He slithered through the garden and
   he slithered through the lawn.
I smiled as I chased him
   but, then I had to frown.
For, that snake that I was chasing...
   that snake...he turned around!
And on that summer day,
   for everyone to see
that snake that I was chasing
    .....was NOW.... chasing me!

Curious

I'm a curious cat. I'm a curious kid.
So, I followed my mother
I watched her – I did.
She woke up quite early
Then, down the stairs came,
Placed the old coffee pot
On the old stove top frame.
She poured that black brew
In her favorite old mug.
"Can I please try it out?"
I asked with a shrug.
With a nod from her head
I slowly walked up.
Took a hold of that mug,
Took a sip from that cup.
Y U C K!!!

Gone

My grandpa died
   the other day.
His soul
   he did surrender.
We know he'd want,
   upon his grave,
These words:

   "Return to sender!"

GLUE

MY MOTHER FILLED MY GLASS WITH GLUE,
    IT LOOKED LIKE MILK TO ME.
I TOOK A COUPLE SWALLOWS
    AND, NOW YOU WILL AGREE,
THAT, I DON'T MAKE NEAR THE NOISE
    THAT ONCE I USED TO MAKE.
I'M GIVING MOTHER'S EARS
    A LONG AWAITED BREAK.
FOR, IT'S HARD TO YELL OR SCREAM
    OR, SING AN OFF-TUNE SONG
WHEN YOUR TEETH ARE STUCK TOGETHER
    WITH GLUE THAT'S SUPER STRONG.
I HAVEN'T SAID A WORD ALL WEEK
    MY MOTHER LOOKS CONTENT.
WHEN MOTHER FILLED MY GLASS WITH GLUE..
    THAT................ WAS HER INTENT!

BEANS

I ate a bunch of beans today –
the kind that make me fart.
I know that I'll be tooting soon.
I wonder when they'll start?
I DO know that they'll probably smell.
I bet they'll stink a bunch.
'Cause, I know my gas, I know it well –
It's more than just a hunch.
But, today I have a brand new plan.
I'll toot when I am walking.
I'll let the gas out slowly,
so, my two buns won't be knocking.
And, though I thought my plan was great,
my friends were rather blunt.
For, while in line, I heard them chime.....
"WE WISH YOU WEREN'T IN FRONT!"

THE SHOT

It's time to get my flu shot.
It's that awful time of year.
The thought of shiny needles,
fills my body full of fear.
But, as I'm waiting, in the line,
feeling like I'm cursed,
I smile at the girls,
and I say...."Ladies first!"

Fried

We played out in the ocean.
  Then, in the sun we dried.
We thought we had a good time.
  But, ouch! We got fried!

Don't!

Mother says, "Don't pick your nose.
Don't PUT those boogers on your clothes.
Don't wipe your snot upon your sleeve."
(It makes her sick. It makes her grieve.)
"Don't cover ground with colored spit."
(It's pretty gross, I must admit.)
All these things, she does... forbid.
"But, Mom," I say, "I'm just a kid!"

WHAT WE LIKE... WHAT WE DON'T

Sliding down a handrail. Climbing up a rope.
Sitting in a bathtub and playing with the soap.
Playing in the sun, with all our strength and might.
Watching falling stars in the darkness of the night.
Making forts in trees, and dreaming lots of dreams.
Eating lots of pizza and chocolate chip ice cream.
Running with our dogs, and riding on our bikes.
      THESE are a FEW things, that we kids like.

Dressing up for pictures and having to sit still.
Staying in our bed all day, when we're feeling ill.
Sitting in a wedding, having grandma kiss our face.
Going through a store, at Mother's TURTLE pace!
Sitting in a car, when I really want to play.
Having to come in just because the sky is gray.
DARK socks on the feet. Shiny shoes that CLICK.
THESE are a FEW things, that make us kids...SICK!

And I think I should know - just listen, my dears,
      For I've been a kid.......... for 43 years!

THE BEST CAKE

Today I'll bake a cake.
It will be the best one ever.
I'll add some *new* ingredients.
They'll be sure to call me clever.
So, I add my favorite fruit,
and I add my favorite candy.
I'm smiling ear to ear,
'cause this cake will be a dandy!
Then, I add my favorite vegetable,
green peas, still in the pod.
And, I add my favorite meat dish,
fish sticks made from cod.
My favorite flower goes in, too
as does my favorite spice.
And, a cup of grain, my favorite,
white California Rice.
I add it all, then add some more,
I don't worry what it's costing.
I cook it up and take a bite...
   uh....I think it needs more frosting!

Backward Billy

Backward Billy Baker
had a problem, quite severe.
What should be first,
what should be last,
to him just wasn't clear.
He'd wake up every morning,
and jump into his shoes.
If asked to dress in order,
he kindly would refuse.
It wouldn't be a problem,
and people wouldn't stare,
if he'd only put a coat on last,
instead of underwear!

Idol

You say you like the way I look.
You like the way I walk.
You say you like the way I sing.
You like the way I talk.
You say you want to be like me,
but, what you never knew,
I'll share my little secret now,
I want to be *LIKE YOU!*

Shaved

Daddy shaved his beard today.
It makes him look so thin.
And my, oh my, you can't deny,
He has a funny chin!

Fishing Trip

My grandpa took me fishing. We sat there all day long.
    We ate our lunch. We took a nap. We even sang a song.
We didn't see a single fish. But, Grandpa kept on talking.
    I listened to his stories, while our little boat was rocking.
When the day was done, he shyly asked if, again, I would go out.
    "Of course I would!" I said - there's no shadow of a trout!

Garbage

What can make the whole house smell
  like old and rotting food?
What can make your stomach turn?
  What can change your mood?
What can make you want to get
  a new high-powered fan?
What can do these things and more?
    It seems the garbage can.....can.

What a Kid

He ran into my backyard
and climbed up all the trees.
Then, frolicked, jumped, jiggled, and dove
in a pile of autumn leaves.
He went swinging on the swing-set.
He went sliding on the slide.
We got into a tickle war -
we laughed until we cried.
We played catch until our arms wore out
and tag and so much more.
I know that in the morning,
my body will be sore.
And, then he did a back-flip!
I guarantee he did.
I can't believe my Grandpa,
he acts just like a kid!

But Dad!

But Dad....
It's much too soon, to go to my room.
It's much too light, and I'll put up a fight.
It's much too early, I'm still so squirrelly.
It's much too hot, my mind will rot.
It's much too scary, and unnecessary.
It's much too dark, is my last remark.

**   Well Son...
It's really no use, to make an excuse
It's time now Ed, to get into bed!!!**

JELLY FISH

I found a little jelly fish.
   I left him out to dry.
Now, he is a SMELLY fish.
   My, oh my, oh my!

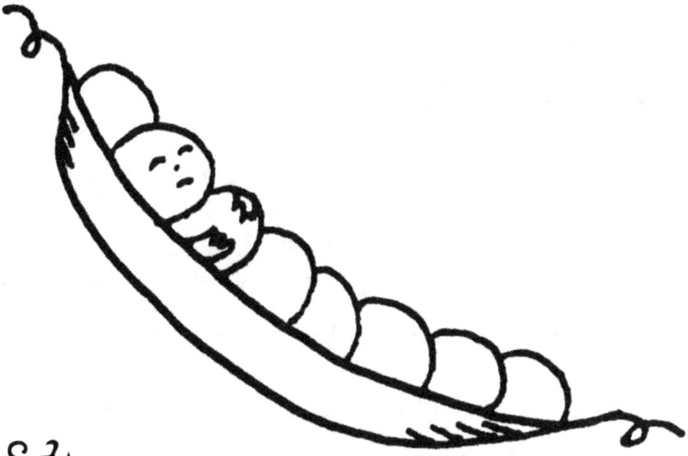

Rest

My grandpa was a farmer.
   One day his heart did cease.
He's buried in a field, now.
   So, he may rest in PEAS!

TOO NEAT
My best friend's hair is slicked back.
  His shoes are shiny, too.
His shirt and pants are always pressed,
  which makes them look brand new.
He makes his bed most everyday.
  He picks up all his clothes.
He never honks, or snorts, or spits
  and doesn't pick his nose!
After working in the yard all day,
  he's sure to wash his feet.
I like this friend but, have to say,
  at times.......he's just TOO NEAT!

Big Belly Bob Yowser Samuel Magee!

Big Belly Bob Yowser Samuel Magee
  is an interesting fellow, just listen you'll see
He's as wide as he's tall and as tall as a house.
  but, big Belly Bob Yowser is as quiet as a mouse.
He'll sit there all day, just twiddling his thumbs.
  But, don't get me wrong, Big Belly Bob's not dumb.
He'll sit there and think, from morning till night
  then, pick up a pen, and furiously write.
He'll write about rockets and far off adventures.
  He'll write about cavities, fillings and dentures.
He'll write about clothes, from the cap to the trouser.
  He's a remarkable man, this Big Belly Bob Yowser.
He can write a love story, that will make a heart melt.
  He can write on forever, on any topic he's dealt.
He'll write a text book, in an hour or two.
  He doesn't like poems but, he's written a few.
Yes, Big Belly Bob Yowser Samuel Magee
  is an interesting fellow, I'm sure you'll agree.
For, he'll write all these things,
  but, won't take the glory.
Except for, maybe, just this one little story.

Big Belly Bob Yowser Samuel Magee - **THAT'S ME!**

OH. MARY.

Mary had a little lamb,
    a little ham, a little jam.
Mary had a little pie,
    a little cake, I don't know why.
And, Mary had a little tea,
    a little milk, and you could see
that Mary got a little squirrely.
    She left the room a little early.
For, she was sad and soon got sadder,
    'cause, Mary had a little bladder.

Mother's Plea

I'll give you a hound if you just quiet down.
I'll give you a jiggle if you just don't giggle.
I'll give you a dollar if you just don't holler.
I'll give you a pie if you just don't cry.
I'll give you a bell if you just won't yell
I'll give you a job if you just won't sob.
I'll give you a missile if you just won't whistle.
I'll give you a ring if you just won't sing.
I'll give you a calf if you just won't laugh
I'll give you a sock if you just won't talk.
I'll give you a kite if you just won't fight.
We'll ride on the bus if you just won't fuss.
I'll start my diet if you just keep quiet.
    Wow.....it's hard to stay calm,
        when you're being a mom!

WHAT THE BOSS SAYS

The applicant entered, with a smile on his face.
    The answer to the question, he knew.
"What's 1 + 1," the company asked.
    "Why of course, the answer is two."
The next person entered, with a confident walk.
    Then, he paused, as he walked through the door.
"What is 2 + 2," the board asked the man.
    "Why folks, the answer is four."
The next lad arrived, and was asked the same thing.
    His response, was that of a whiz.
"The answer to that, there's no doubt in my mind,
    it's whatever the boss... says it is!"
And, so this young man, who's first name was Bob
                           ......GOT THE JOB!

Pie Spy

I spied the pie,
and bless my soul,
I grabbed it up
and swallowed it whole!
Halfway down,
just my luck,
that pumpkin pie,
well, it got stuck!

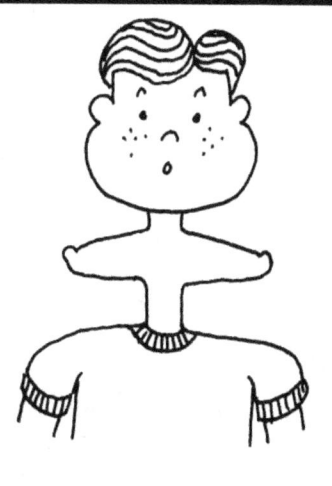

Thumb

I suck my thumb.
I'm not ashamed.
For, MY thumb is the best!
It's long and soft
and tastes so sweet.
It's true. I do not jest.
And, though my thumb
is really great,
I have to say I'm blessed.
For, ALL my fingers
are quite nice.
That's why I suck the rest!

Engineer

One day in May,
I went to work,
and built myself a boat.
I put it in the water and
it wouldn't even float.
Then, in June, at half past noon,
I built myself a car.
The engine is my doggy so,
it doesn't go too far.
Now in July, I do not lie,
I built myself a plane.
Just how they get these things to fly,
I really can't explain!
I've worked so hard.
I've worked so long.
But, this is what I fear.
I might be good at writing,
but, I'm not an engineer!

CRAYONS

Sixty-four crayons. Shiny and new.
    I hope and pray I don't lose 'em.
I don't want them broken - don't want them to shrink.
    So, my thought is...I never should use 'em.
I like how they feel. I like how they smell.
    I like how they look in the box.
When the teacher says "color," and I tell her "NO,"
    Is this what you call...a PARADOX?
My crayons and I...are one in the same.
    If you think we are crazy, just tell us.
Until then, relax and stare at my wax.
    And, admit that You really are JEAL.OUS!!

Plot of Land

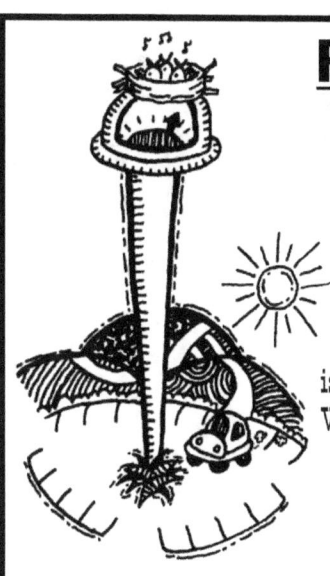

There used to be big trees here.
We'd play among them all.
You should have seen the colors,
when the leaves began to fall.
And the trees, they would provide us
with some shade when it got hot.
But, the only thing we see now,
is this metered parking lot!
Whoever bought
    this lot
        ought not
            .....come around!

Dino

I brought a brontosaurus home.
His head scraped on the door.
I guess that I would have to say,
He has a **Dino-SORE!**

Picture Perfect Patty

Picture perfect Patty,
is the snobby, bratty sort.
Though her face is darn near perfect,
her temperament is short.
She has a perfect smile,
but, it seems she always frowns,
She seems to get her kicks,
from putting others down.
Her hair is brown. Her nose is straight.
Her eyes ...a gorgeous blue.
But, like I said, she's snobby,
So, for friends she has but few.
So, for this gal, I took it on,
to give her some advice:
"It's nice that you are pretty,
but, we'd rather have you nice!"

NELLA

Nella's umbrella was dainty and cute.
    But, then again, Nella was, too.
She wore dainty dresses and cute little gloves.
    And, goodness, just look at those shoes.
One day she was walking. It started to rain.
    She used the umbrella that day.
The wind was quite strong. I wish I was wrong.
    But, Nella just floated away!
It's hard to believe, so hard to believe,
    the umbrella was part of her fate.
But, so was the wind and so was the rain,
    and so was her size and her weight!
So, if you are skinny, and walking outdoors,
    and sense a storm in the air......
    ....beware!!!

Little Brother?

I'm taller than my brother now.
When I show him, he erupts!
'Cause instead of GETTING hand-me-downs,
I'm GIVING hand-me UPS!

The Comma

The comma is in the world
for one important cause
It makes whoever's reading,
pause!

SHOPPING STRESS

I couldn't find the toothpaste,
    and where'd they put the candy?
The soda's with the cereal.
    That doesn't seem too handy!
The coffee's with the pickles
    and the pudding's with the prunes!
There's a canister of helium,
    but, I can't find ONE balloon!
They've plum run out of hot dogs!
    I can't take it any more!
It's no wonder that they named this,
    the <u>IN</u>convenient store!

Revenge

I'm going to see my girlfriend.
I'm mad at her, I am.
So, in a glass I put
one juicy, slimy clam.
I add to it some garlic,
and a dash of pickle juice
horseradish and Tabasco,
and sprig of grounded spruce.
I chop up a red onion,
then, I mix it all around.
I open up my mouth,
and, slowly drink it down.
So, when we get together,
she will make a quick diagnosis
that I'm getting back at her,
with a case of halitosis!

Get up!

My mother said, "It can't be done."
    My father said, "Yeah, right!"
My brother said, "Hey, get a clue."
    He COULD be more polite.
My friends they said, there's just no way.
    They said it with a sneer.
I COULD nod yes. I COULD agree.
    And, that's my biggest fear.
When people don't believe in you,
    they think you cannot win,
You feel like you've been beaten down...
    Get up! Get up, again!

Why I Like You

It's not your muscles,
It's not your clothes.
It's not your eyes,
It's not your nose.
It's not your smile,
  with teeth so white.
It's not your weight.
It's not your height.
It's not your knowledge.
It's not your job.
It's not your serve.
It's not your lob.
It's not your money.
It's not your fame.
I'm sorry to say,
  it's not your name.
It's not your house.
It's not your car.
It's what's inside.
It's who you are.

Friends

There will always be struggles,
but, I think in the end,
I can always get by,
with help from my friends.

The Face

I woke up in the morning,
    a strange face, I do see.
I squint to see it better.
    He's squinting back at me.
The face is all contorted.
    It must be from distress.
He tries to fix his hair,
    but, it's too much of a mess.
I try to look away,
    but, my vision starts to clear.
And once again I realize,
    I'm looking in a mirror!

Rich

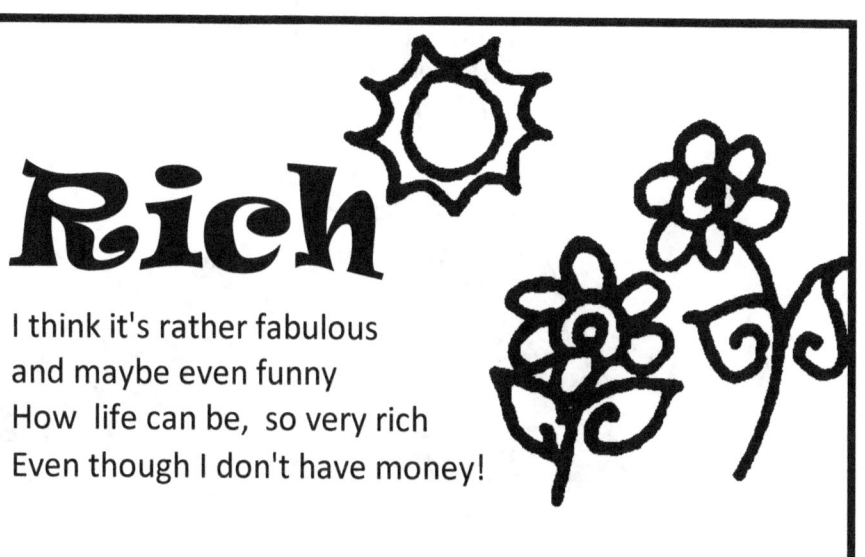

I think it's rather fabulous
and maybe even funny
How life can be, so very rich
Even though I don't have money!

ARE WE THERE YET?

Traveling down the road,
I'm feeling rather antsy.
I'm getting kind of hungry.
I'd like a burger, nothing fancy.
Then, I feel the need,
to roll the window down.
"Tell me who just tooted!"
I'm saying with a frown.
Traveling down the road,
my seat is getting sore.
It makes me mad to think,
we've got a hundred miles more.
Billy has to go, for the 32nd time.
Susie wants a coke, Mom, a lemon-lime.
The dog starts barking,
the kids begin to shout,
that hitchhiker's wanting in,
but, for me, I'm wanting out!
Yes, traveling down the road,
and you can surely bet
that everyone is asking....
"...ARE WE THERE YET?!"

PARADE

There's a parade coming through.
 It's colorful.   It's bright.
There's a parade coming through.
 Oh, what a sight!
You shouldn't dare miss this.
It's right on our street.
Just sit on your porches.
You'll have the best seat.
There's a parade coming through.
 Everyone come see!
Even if it's just......
...my puppy and me!

Gifts

Don't count the money, that I spent.
Nor count the gifts, I bought.
I ask of you, to think it through,
and please just count the thought!

CRYBABY

My brother started crying.
He couldn't seem to stop.
At first we used a handkerchief.
Then, we used a mop.
My mother got her wading boots.
I stood up on a stool.
We took him to our backyard and,
he filled our swimming pool!
The tears, they kept on flowing,
and the river took its course.
No one could believe,
that my brother was the source.
And, though this crying problem,
is a problem that I dread,
I'm glad my little brother,
has never wet the bed!

TIME FOR ME!

Ok, I need to know...
    are you finished with your show?
Did you sing your song
    and dance your dance?
Are you ready now to go?
    So, finish, please. Oh, hurry.
So, the audience can see,
    In the spotlight, in the limelight,
will now be me, me, me!

Early Bird

The early bird gets the worm.
The late bird gets the bread.
My advice, sleep in late.
And, take the toast instead.

Mary's Pets

Mary had a little CLAM,
    whose insides were like jelly.
And, everywhere that Mary went,
    we knew, cause it was smelly!
She took the clam to school one day.
    The kids? They plugged their noses!
She asked to keep it there all day.
    The teacher? She opposes!
She took it home at lunch time,
    then, brought back her pet spider.
The teacher took one look at it,
    and said, "Would you please hide her?"
The next day Mary brought to school,
    her little silver snake.
While backing up, the teacher said,
    "OUT, for Heaven's sake!"
And, in the days that followed,
    she always brought a pet.
Each day her teacher rolled her eyes,
    and nervously would fret.
But, finally on a winter day,
    her teacher, she did please.
She brought a little lamb,
    with snow white, silky fleece.
Hmmm.
  Maybe I should write a poem about that...
    Mary had a little lamb...

Darla

Darla drank some water.
    Then, she drank some pop.
She drank a little milk
    and, she couldn't seem to stop!
She drank a little fruit juice.
    She wiggled to and fro.
Look out, everybody!
    Darla's gotta GO!

Inch by Inch

I tried to do too much today
    It made my stomach kink.
I tried to do too much today,
    and here is what I think:
That...by the yard, life is hard,
    and, now I know it's true,
That...inch by inch, life's a cinch.
    I've learned it, how 'bout you?

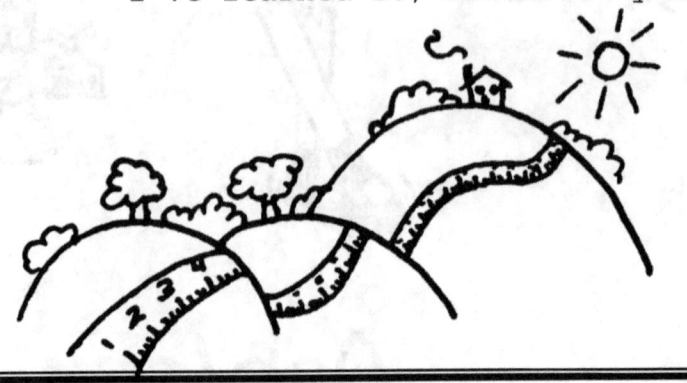

Seattle Dreams

Somewhere in this great big world,
    it's sunny and it's warm.
There are people lying on a beach,
    tanning legs and tanning arms.
They're swimming in their swimming trunks.
    They're playing in the sun.
In cut off shirts and cut off pants,
    they're having so much fun.
Yes, somewhere it's a summer day,
    and, it's driving me insane.
'Cause, here I sit inside my house,
    staring......at the rain!

CHOICES

You like being inside - I like being out.
You like water from a glass - I like it from a spout.
Some people like to spend - some are rather frugal.
Some are shy about success - some blow it like a bugle,
Some, choose to go to church - some choose to pray alone.
Some choose to talk all day, upon their telephone.
Some like to have short hair - others choose it long.
Some, choose to write a book - while others write a song.
Some want to be a doctor - others want to teach.
Others choose to play all day... upon a sandy beach.
Some prefer to follow - others like to lead.
While some are busy cutting trees - others plant the seed.
Some will order French fries - some like onion rings.
Some will choose to eat, the strangest, weirdest things.
This is coming to an end so, I'll have to raise my voice.
There are many options in this world,
AREN'T YOU GLAD YOU HAVE A CHOICE!?!?

WHAT I'VE GOT

I don't have a hammer. I don't have a nail.
I don't have a mop. I don't have a pail.
I don't have paper, scissors or glue.
Snd, staples and paper clips, I have but a few.
I don't have much but, I have a great thought
I'll do my best - with whatever I've got.

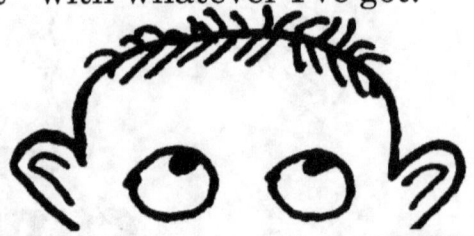

Minds are like parachutes - they only function when open.
Dreams are like good luck - they start with some hopin'.
Friendship's like learning - it only happens when trying.
Smiles are like sunsets - they're free for the buying.
Promises are like glass - they're easily broken.
Faces are like pictures - they say things, with nothing spoken.
Living is like cheese - it gets better with age.
I hope that you've learned, from the words on this page.

Shorties

Do you think this poem is too short, my friend?
THE END

This poem is short but, some say it's fun.
Oh, by the way, it's done.

This poem is short, it's not long, it's not tall
That's all.

I think this poem's lines are too few.
Do you?

This poem is short and that's no lie
Good-Bye!

This poem is short and probably a bore.
Fortunately...there's no more.

This poem's rather short. I could write to make it grow
But....no.

This poem is short. It's a truth, I confess.
That's all......I guess.

Backward Poet

A backward poet, they say I am.
 I fear it is a curse.
For, whenever I write a poem or two
 I always write...INVERSE.

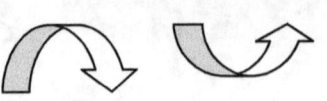

Good News!

My mom rushed in with keys in hand.
 Her face...a smile? A smirk?
"The good news first!", she said to Dad,
 "Those air-bags... really work!"

FOREVER

I want to live forever.
 If I can, I think I should.
My mother says there's just no way.
 But, hey....so far - so good!

DIET

On the third day of my diet
 I felt ...thinner and fit.
So, on the third day of my diet
 ....I QUIT!

No Sunshine

A day without sunshine...
    the analogy started
What ending could be the remark?
    A day without sunshine?
So much I could say.
    But, a day without sunshine....is DARK

Puzzle

I'm feeling overly smart today.
    I'm proud and just a bit smug.
When mom finds out and tells my dad.
    I'm SURE they'll give me a hug.
They'll jump for joy and clap their hands
    and proudly shed a tear.
For, I finished that puzzle in less than a week...
    when the box said 3 to 5 years!

FARMER

A farmer threw milk and cheese at me.
    I dodged it all..... just barely!
I thought it so disgusting that,
    I had to say... "How DAIRY!"

WORD TO THE WISE

"Here's a word to the WISE"

That's what the sign said.

Now, I know I must be concise.

Does it make sense to you

that the WISE need a clue?

It's the STUPIDS that need the advice!

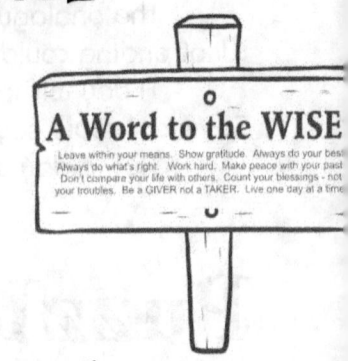

MEAL TIME

Mommas plan for meal time,
at times I had to grieve it.
The only choice she ever gave,
was take the food
...or LEAVE IT!

Sleep

Sleeping comes so naturally.
Yes, I'm bragging as I say,
I can do this thing called sleeping
With my eyes closed - all the way!

Weatherman

I think I'll be a weatherman.
    I'll try my skills right now.
I WON'T...tell you my secrets.
    So, PLEASE...don't ask me how.
But, here is my prediction.
    It's not just a whim or a lark.
My meteorological conclusion
    Tonight..... it's going to be... DARK.

HUH?

My teacher is downright confusing!
Her directions don't seem to make sense.
At times she'll ask in the present...
but, mostly it's all in past tense.
And *when,* we line up for walking,
it can be a ridiculous sight.
'Cause, she always tells us to line up,
by last name according to height!

Fool

A fool and his money are parted,
    as quickly, as quickly can be.
But, how did they FIRST get together?
    THAT's what's not clear to me!

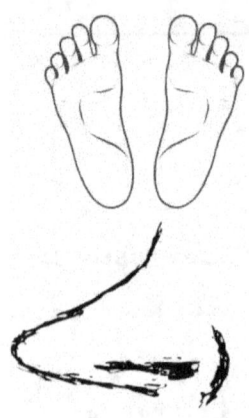

Brother

My brother was built a bit backwards.
    His nose and his toes are reversed.
You can call it a little bit funny.
    I call it a terrible curse.
Though his nostrils can do all the sniffing,
    it's his toes that know how to SMELL!
His feet go walking and jogging,
    and, it's his NOSE that RUNS really well!

Uncle William

Uncle WILLIAM joined the army
    and, he did the usual things -
did the push-ups, did the running,
    and, while marching - he did sing.
He did it all - he did it well,
    he did his best...until,
the sergeant at the firing range,
    said, "Ready...fire at WILL!"

NIGHT OUT

I took a prune to dinner -
    saw a movie - stayed out late.
I took a prune to dinner,
    'cause, I couldn't find... a date!

PONY

My pony was not feeling well -
    I knew she was running a fever.
Her cough was like a Mac truck -
    I knew I couldn't just leave her.
She coughed through the night
                  till morn.
    Her neigh was soft, of course.
So, now my Shetland pony...
    is just a little... hoarse.

DEAD SEA

While traveling abroad, we came to a sign
    "This way to see - the Dead Sea".
My father looked grim and scratched his bald head,
    He said, "Now how can this be?"
He shook his head hard and let out a sigh
    "This must be, must be, a trick.
But, if it is true, I hadn't a clue....
    I didn't even know it was sick!"

Not Feeling Well

My mother says I caught a cold.
   It's true, my throat is sore.
But, the fact that I am burning up,
   is what I can't ignore.
I'm sweating from head to toes.
   It's making me distraught.
My mother says I caught a cold.
   I think I caught a HOT!

Stay Home Dad

My daddy lost his job last week.
   and, though it is a shame,
Now that he is home so much,
   he finally knows my name!

Left Gone

I can't tell you when it happened
   but, it happened - yes indeed.
My whole **LEFT** side just disappeared -
   I didn't cry or bleed.
But, here I am with no left side -
   It MUST be quite a sight!
When people ask if I'm okay...
   I tell them...I'm ALL RIGHT

The End.

Alphabetical Index

Advice 20
Advice for Santa 91
Allowance 118
Are We There Yet? 160

Baby Sit 44
Bath 85
Back to Bed 87
Backward Billy 138
Backward Poet 172
Baseball Bumble 9
Be Nice 58
Beans 133
Believe 45
Better Pets 77
Big Belly Bob Yowser 145
Blue Lagoon 31
Boo 17
Brand New Marker 53
Broccoli 125
Brother 19
Brother 176
But Dad 142
Bye 27

Cannot Sleep 65
Careful 55
Cats 68
Choices 167
Christmas Wish 90
Cloud 9 99
Contest 24
Crayons 150
Crisis in Class 101
Crybaby 162
Curious 131

Dad's Beard 116
Dare Devil 111
Darla 165

Dead Sea 176
Decorating 94
Diet 107
Diet 172
Dinner 28
Dinner Joke 114
Dinner Dilemma 125
Dino 151
Dog Decisions 67
Dog Gone 66
Dogs 66
Don't 135
Don't be Afraid 79
Don't Lose It 29
Donny's Desk 100
Doughnuts 46
Dreams, Screams
 & Jelly Beans 6

Early Bird 163
Early Gift 95
Engineer 149
Epitaph 31
Ever? 11

Farmer 173
Fishing Trip 140
Fool 175
Forever 172
Fried 134
Friend 25
Friends 158

Gaggle of Geese 73
Garbage 140
Germ 105
Get Down 63
Get Up 157
Gifts 161

Glue	132
Golf	82
Gone	131
Good / Bad	43
Good Learners	80
Good News	172
Grandma's Gone	52
Green Bananas	126
Gunny Grin	23

Hair	82
Happy Hydrant	62
Hello, My Friend	15
Help	103
High Dive Dilemma	21
Holiday News	91
Homework	103
Homonym Scholar	109
Horse	74
Horses	70
How Would You React?	35
Hugs	88
Huh?	175
Humpty	41
Humpty 2	41
Hungry	128

I Can?	60
I feel Like Playing in Mud	61
I Cream	14
Idol	139
Inch by Inch	166

Jack & Jill	50
Jelly Fish	143
Jimmy Zat	22
Johnny Joe	32
Joy	36

Ketchup	40

Laugh	65
Left Gone	178
Life's an Adventure	27
Life's Too Short	26
Lion	16
Listen	121
Little Brother?	154
Lollipop	117
Love & Lies	102

Magic Bro	112
Mary's Pets	164
Mealtime	115
Mealtime	174
Minds	168
Mom's Working	117
Money	54
Morning Chore	123
Mother's Plea	146
Move It	86
My Pet Hen	62
My Way	78

Nella	153
New Kitten	72
Night Out	177
No Artist	81
No Hair	105
No Luck	39
No Twin	124
No Sunshine	173
Not Feeling Well	177
Not-So-Funny-Bone	113

Oh, Mary	146
Okay	12
On Aging	37

Parade

Parakeet	71
Past Tense	8
Pet Problems	71
Picture Perfect Patty	152
Pie Spy	147
Plan	7
Plan to Plan	98
Plans	58
Plot of Land	151
Polite	47
Pony	176
Porcupine	63
Pumpkin Time	89
Puzzle	173
Python	54

Question	49
Questions	50

Rain	49
Rest	143
Revenge	156
Rich	159
Rip City	33
Roof Top	13
Room Clean	129
Room Cleaning	38
Room Gloom	111
Rude	64
Rules	98

Salsa	23
Sandwich Club	34
Seattle Dreams	166
Secret	114

Shaved	139
Shopping Stress	155
Shorties	169
Show Me	56
Sick	127
Sleep	174
Slow Going	96
Smart Dog	69
Smart Kid	18
Snake	69
Sneezy	127
Spider	75
Stay Home Dad	178
Step on a Crack	122
Still Me?	119
Stone Soup	124
Success	106
Sweet Lesson	86
Sword Swallower	110

Talk	48
Tarantula	51
Teacher's Last Lecture	100
Telephone Moan	123
The Best Cake	137
The Chase	130
The Chicken and the Human	76
The Christmas Tree	93
The Comma	154
The Face	159
The Greatest Fault	104
The Scare	59
The Season	90
The Shot	134
The Ump	10
Thief	10
Things	57
Thumb	148
Time for Me	163
Tis the Season	92
To The Teacher	57
Too Much	78

Too Neat	144
Too Sick	40
Try	120
Two-Headed Dog	30

U̲ncle William   176
Under Talk   36

V̲omit   97

W̲alrus   70
Weatherman	175
Wedgy	84
What a Kid	141
What I've Got	168
What the Boss Says	147
What We Like…	136
Why I Like You	158
Wise Teacher	42
Wish	83
Wishing	22
Word to the Wise	174
Would You Rather	46

Z̲ukes   108

Other Publications from
Missing Piece Press, LLC

Thinking Books
Thinklers! 1
Thinklers! 2
Thinklers! 3
Science Stumpers
Algebra Summary Sheets
Number Wonders
History Mysteries

Children's Books
Reindolphins

Board Games
WHEW!
ShanJari

Card Games
TooT!
Blam!
Word Nerd
State Debate

Dice Games
DICE Blam!

A Little Thinking...a LOT of FUN!™

MissingPiecePress.com
Follow us on FaceBook!

www.ingramcontent.com/pod-product-compliance
Lightning Source LLC
Chambersburg PA
CBHW050638300426
44112CB00012B/1842